Family Law Matters

Law and Social Theory
A Pluto series

Series editor PETER FITZPATRICK
Professor of Law and Social Theory, University of Kent

Dangerous Supplements
EDITED BY PETER FITZPATRICK

The Critical Lawyers' Handbook
EDITED BY IAN GRIGG-SPALL AND PADDY IRELAND

The Wrongs of Tort
JOANNE CONAGHAN AND WADE MANSELL

Forthcoming

Land Law: A Critical Supplement
NICK JACKSON

Trusts: A Critical Commentary
ROGER COTTERRELL

Contract: A Critical Supplement
JOHN WIGHTMAN

Law in the Information Society
ANDREW CLARK AND ABDUL PALIWALA

FAMILY LAW MATTERS

Katherine O'Donovan

Pluto  Press

LONDON • BOULDER, COLORADO

First published 1993 by Pluto Press
345 Archway Road, London N6 5AA
and 5500 Central Avenue
Boulder, Colorado 80301, USA

British Library Cataloguing in Publication Data
A Catalogue record for this book is available from the British Library
ISBN 0 7453 0506 7 hb
ISBN 0 7453 0507 5 pb

Library of Congress Cataloging in Publication Data
A catalog record is available from the Library of Congress

Designed and Produced for Pluto Press by
Chase Production Services, Chipping Norton
Typeset from author's disks by
Stanford Desktop Publishing Services, Milton Keynes
Printed in Great Britain by T.J. Press, Padstow

For JD and JFD
who agreed to
a year of my own

Contents

Acknowledgements

This book was written during the academic year 1991–92 during which time I was a Jean Monnet fellow at the European University Institute, Florence. My thanks to Professor Brian Bercusson of the Department of Juridical Sciences and to Professor Heinz-Gerhard Haupt of the European Cultural Centre for their support. The staff of the library at the Institute were unfailingly courteous and helpful. The University of Kent Law School gave me leave from my duties there, and its Research Committee provided a grant towards the production of the text. Particular thanks to three friends from Kent who helped with the book: Anne Bottomley who read and advised with insight and charm; Peter Fitzpatrick who as editor of this series has encouraged and cajoled; and Freda Vincent who took charge of the manuscript with cheerfulness and efficiency. I am also indebted to Mariana Von Benson, one of my former students, who prepared the index and checked the text with kindness, and to Michael King for his comments on Chapter 6. Christine Considine of Pluto Press is the considerate and thorough copy editor who prepared the text for publication. The manuscript was delivered to the publishers in May 1992 and it has not been possible to incorporate legal developments since then.

During my time in Florence I took part in the Women's Studies Inter-disciplinary Seminar organised by Yota Kravariton and by Olwyn Hufton and in the seminar entitled 'Social Contracts: Old and New', organised by Steven Lukes, and by Veronica Munoz-Darde and Maurice Glasman. Much of the way I now see family law has been influenced by arguments in and out of the seminar with the organisers, and with Sally Sheldon, Julia Sohrab, Barbara MacLennon, Verena Stolcke, Jeff Weintraub, Alastair Davidson, Adrian Favell, Deirdre Boden, David Purdy, Catherine Neveu, and others.

Any author's proceeds from the sale of this book will be given to Amnesty International.

Table of Statutes

Table of Cases

Introduction

What do writers forget when they write books on the subject we call family law? Are they organisers and synthesisers of the material or do they merely record what courts and legislators say? That is a question to which this book is addressed. If the role of the writer is active, then it is likely that books, even legal textbooks, are written from a point of view. This necessarily implies overlooking other points of view. The series of which *Family Law Matters* forms a part proposes to identify and record the voices of those excluded from other textbooks; to find and document aspects of law that have been forgotten or ignored. Criticism of legal writing for taking too narrow a view of law is not justly made where family law is concerned. Academic writers on family and law do not belong to the expository tradition of English law from which the broader context of culture, society and the economy is excluded. This is not a 'closed' area, written about only as positive law; it was one of the first areas in the law curriculum to become interested in socio-legal perspectives. Yet there is still place for a book which opens up questions about family law in a way that traditional textbooks and casebooks cannot. That is the object of *Family Law Matters*. It is a book of perspectives.

Too often law books present law in a 'take it or leave it' fashion. The active role of those who produce law in practice and law in books is not openly acknowledged. All of us, including readers, are engaged in a process of constructing knowledge. One of the ideas of this book is to engage the reader in conversation, to catch the reader's attention, to stimulate and even to annoy the reader. I am looking for debate, disagreement, dispute. This is because I believe that, like other writers on law, I am not just a recorder but an organiser who makes choices about what to include. The ways in which legal material is presented to readers, the emphases on particular aspects, are not pre-ordained. Just as judges and other law makers are faced with choices, so too are academic writers, in my view.

Family law is dynamic; it is in flux. But it is embedded in the legal tradition from which it springs. I have tried to reflect this in my writing. Chapter 1 opens with a case study of how family law is produced and how it changes. The idea is to empower the reader to question, to get behind, seemingly immutable tradition. It is not enough simply to denounce legal rules or precedents as wrong, discriminatory, unfair. They may very well be so, but to alter them we need to understand where they come from, what they stand for, how they are represented, how they change. Otherwise we may be faced with institutional justifications which are used to inhibit change. The story of the marital rape exemption in this chapter is designed to show how hard it is to bring alternative viewpoints into the light; and yet how quickly things can alter once a new way of seeing is developed. The English legal tradition is one of continuity. Change is therefore hard to account for, and open acknowledgement undermines continuity. One way in which change is officially explained is by maintaining that the particular alteration is part of continuity; that its origins lie in existing precedents. In a sense this must necessarily be so. But the denial of change can also be puzzling. The first chapter intends to explain how this process occurs. It is designed to alert readers to possibilities of new perspectives within the existing rules. It looks for a response which refuses to accept the answer: 'that is the law; that is how things are.'

Chapter 2 intends to make readers ask themselves about family law as a subject both in the law curriculum and in practice. Who are the producers? How are the boundaries delimited? What kinds of people become judges of the Family Division of the High Court? What sort of legal education is available to legal practitioners, particularly to those who make the law? What assistance is given to those who must judge and who claim to speak for others in understanding those others and their experiences? How is the subject family law defined in the academy? What means have been devised by academic writers to present their subject? In what ways do those of us writing about the law fail our readers?

The point of Chapter 3 is to pose the question of persons subject to family law. Which types of family are recognised and legitimated by law? Which types of family are denied legal approval? Does it matter? The chapter goes on to ask why some relationships are privileged by legal acknowledgement and what the features of these relationships are. Answers given suggest an ideology of the family, which the writer criticises as being against liberty and equality, and which some readers may not wish to uphold. At the same time we are faced with the question about other long-term relationships, between same-sex partners for example, of how to nominate these, if not as families.

Chapter 4 tackles a family law staple – marriage. For me the interesting issue is why we remain so attached to an institution which seems to defy the deconstructive efforts of many writers. Because arguments based on self-interest and rationality touch only the surface of human behaviour, myth, tradition and continuity provide a means of analysis an alternative reading for this chapter. This does not mean that I accept the exclusion of those who are denied participation in the mythology; nor that I believe that socio-legal institutions can be justified in such terms. The mythic content arises from cultural traditions which pose problems for those who do not share those traditions. There are other ways of seeing, as examples from European countries such as Denmark and Sweden illustrate. There is an aspect to this which calls on the recently developed European tradition of human rights as a standard whereby we may criticise existing institutional definitions and provisions for enduring human relationships. In that way the writing of this chapter attempts to stand outside marriage as an institution and to examine it from an external viewpoint. The power that law has, in its language, in the way it structures our way of seeing, cannot be understood from inside. We have to stand outside in order to understand that coercion may be about vision, our capacity to see. At the same time, by standing outside we assert control over language, over argument, over law's way of thinking and talking.

Chapter 5 deepens this analysis with a specific focus on the ways in which gender is inscribed in family law. This chapter and Chapter 6 reverse the question of what the subject family law is, and ask instead *who* is the subject of family law. The argument is advanced that the subject is a gendered adult; that family law cannot conceive of a genderless subject, nor of a child subject; and that children are objects but not subjects of law. Underlying this is a clear judgement that the construction of a gendered adult subject, and the denial of subjectivity to children, are restrictions on individual liberty. The charge that these structures are sources of inequality is also maintained. Again the method is one of standing outside, of checking law's power to define against ideals of equality and liberty. The recovery of the stories of those people whose individuality is erased in generalised legal rules, the bringing of their stories into the light, is upheld as a requirement for justice.

Finally, Chapter 7 places family law in a wider debate about political theory. The failure of political philosophy to theorise the family, and the consequent maintenance of the position that it is a natural unit, are presented as failings within the dominant philosophy of liberalism. Not only does this neglect the ways in which the family is created and recreated as a social and legal institution, but it involves a myopia which can be interpreted as self-interested. Political philosophy has been largely written by men, whose vision may be limited by their lack of involvement in the daily care for others in the household. The claim to stand outside existing institutions and to ask whether they can be justified is made by political philosophers. The charge of a failure to theorise the family is a serious one against a discipline which claims impartiality, and neutrality. Theorisation of the family as an institution, as we shall see in this book, leaves present legal and social structures open to the criticism of discrimination between persons on grounds of ascribed characteristics, that is, qualities of birth. Further-more, these institutional structures deny choice of terms of membership without coherent justification. Lastly, I advance my version of the rela-tionship between citizenship and family, but leave it open to readers to draw their own conclusions about the place of the family in the wider world of state and civil society. My view is that liberals' failure to theorise the family must lead us to certain conclusions about liberalism and its ability to deal with ethical questions.

My idea of this book is that it creates space for thought and dis-agreement. It is true that the choice of material and the way it is presented reflect my own preoccupations and values. But I have tried not to be too dogmatic. The shape I have created and the language I have used cannot be neutral, but neither are the shapes and languages of other textbooks and casebooks, as I see them. Above all I have tried to be honest with my readers, but to persuade them, while leaving open the choice of whether to agree with me or not. If my readers respond in the way of those students of family law who have delighted and challenged me over the years with their insight, knowledge, questions, and refusal to accept conventional answers, I shall be content.

1
How Family Law is Produced

The story of the marital rape exemption, which follows, is a story of the immunity of husbands from the criminal law despite a serious sexual assault on a woman, a wife. Although it may seem that criminal law is in issue, it is the status of the female victim as wife which provides the explanation for immunity. In that sense this is a story of family law.

My reason for starting with a story is that I want readers to ask themselves how law, which has an 'is' quality, can change. How does a seemingly immutable rule, which is stated and re-stated by the courts, suddenly disappear? And if one significant rule can be changed, might further change yet be possible?

A Case Study Based on Marital Rape Exemption

Sir Matthew Hale CJ in 1736 published a compilation of law drawn from his court experiences, entitled *Pleas of the Crown*. At that time there were few written sources of law and little judicial authority on rape generally. Hale's views were influential, despite originating in a book rather than in a formal source of law such as a precedent case or statute. Hale declared: 'The husband cannot be guilty of a rape committed by himself upon his lawful wife, for by their mutual matrimonial consent and contract the wife hath given up herself in this kind unto her husband which she cannot retract' (1736, vol 1: 629). What made Hale come to this conclusion? The only relevant previous reported case was that in which the Earl of Castlehaven had been convicted after he held down his wife to enable 'one of his minions' to rape her, *Lord Audley's Case* (1631). Hale could have looked to this case as a precedent for a husband's liability for rape of his wife. Instead he interpreted it as concerning rape by a stranger, with the husband convicted of rape as a principal in the second degree. The wife was admitted as a witness against her husband, although this was opposed by his lawyers.

When Hale came to compile the law of rape there was little written material available. As Temkin (1987: 44) explains: 'He would have been able to look at Bracton and the medieval law as well as at Lord Castlehaven's case. Faced with such a dearth of modern authority Hale had plenty of scope to steer the law in a different direction and this, to some extent, he did.' But although he acknowledged that a concubine's departure from cohabitation was a withdrawal of consent, thus differing

1

from the medieval law position, he argued that a wife was in a different position, because of her consent to marriage; so he retained the medieval line for married women but not for concubines. Temkin (1987: 45) concludes: 'Hale's choice to retain the medieval approach to consent in the case of married women only was to shape the course of the law up to the present day.'

This brief history does not of itself explain why subsequent courts accorded such reverence to Hale's opinion. The explanation must lie not so much with Hale himself but with the legal mentality. An issue that was open at the time of Hale's writing becomes closed once the written word appears. Yet today the past existence of what came to be called the marital rape exemption is characterised (in the House of Lords) a 'fiction' , *R* v. *R* (1991). Not only did Hale create law in his text, but each time that text was accepted as authoritative it constituted another law-making act. And when the 'fiction' was so termed, law was made again. What we see is a threefold process. A statement in an informal source – a book – is accepted by a court as law. This case becomes a precedent for other cases; it is now a formal source of law. When it is termed a 'fiction' over two centuries later it loses its authority as law.

A reading of *Lord Audley's Case* (1631) juxtaposed with a reading of Hale's *Pleas of the Crown* (1736) shows a clever sleight of pen. In the former there was no discussion of eternal consent to sexual inter-course in marriage. The question was not raised. The status of a married woman, and whether she could bear witness against her husband, attracted legal argument, but the court allowed her to do so as 'the party grieved and on whom the crime is committed' (1631: 414). This was an unusual acknowledgement of a wife's autonomy. Turning to Hale's text, what do we find? First the author asserts the general proposition about the mutual matrimonial consent and contract whereby the wife has given up her body to her husband *in perpetuum*. In the next paragraph *Lord Audley's Case* is discussed. There Hale acknowledges that a husband, present at a rape who aids and assists is guilty as a principal 'altho the wife cannot have an appeal of rape against her husband, yet he is indictable for it at the King's suit ...' And the rapist is also guilty 'notwithstanding the husband assisted in it, for tho in marriage she hath given up her body to her husband she is not to be by him prostituted to another.' But the positive statements of a wife's lack of power are not to be found in the original case. They are a gloss placed by Hale – part of his interpretation, or his reading of the case, which he fits into his proposition about a wife's consent. An alternative reading is that a wronged or abused wife can have her husband indicted for rape (1631: 401, 402).

This story might have ended with Hale had it not been for the reverence accorded to his text by subsequent judges. The fiction of a wife's permanent consent to sexual intercourse with her husband was based on a myth created by Hale. And that myth acquired the status of legal doctrine because of the sacred character of Hale's text. Subsequent courts did not ask the source of Hale's assertion. For most judges it was sufficient to find the source in Hale's book. But divergent views were expressed. For example, in *Clarence* (1888) some doubt was cast as follows: 'The authority of Hale CJ on such a matter is undoubtedly as high as any can be, but no other authority is cited by him for this proposition ...' (Field, J in *Clarence* (1888: 57)). Several judges suggested that violent sexual intercourse imposed by a husband could be a crime where the wife's health was endangered.

Hale's authority was challenged more directly by Wills J who argued that there are circumstances in which marital intercourse can be rape 'unless, indeed as between married persons rape is impossible, a proposition to which I certainly am not prepared to assent and for which there seems to me to be no sufficient authority' *Clarence* (1888: 31). But as so often with English law, we find seeming contradiction. Thus Hawkins J could not 'conceive it possible seriously to doubt that a wife would be justified in resisting by all means in her power, nay, even to the death, if necessary, the sexual embraces of a husband suffering from [such] contagious disorder [as gonorrhoea]' (1888: 51). But he was firm on the matrimonial privilege, assering several times:

> This wife submits to her husband's embraces because at the time of the marriage she gave him an irrevocable right to her person. The intercourse which takes place between husband and wife after marriage is not by virtue of any special consent on her part, but is mere submission to an obligation imposed on her by law. Consent is immaterial.

The subsequent story concentrates on the everlasting nature of a wife's consent. Gradually the courts stated one small exception after another: a separation order from the courts revoked consent in *Clarke* (1949); a decree nisi, the preliminary court order for divorce, in *O'Brien* (1974); an undertaking by the husband to a court not to enter the nurses' home where the wife was living, nor to assault, molest nor interfere with her in *Steele* (1977); a formal deed of separation coupled with a court order of non-molestation in *Roberts* (1986). As these 'exceptions' to the rule of everlasting consent show, the principle was not challenged. Indeed it was confirmed, the male marital right was upheld, but legal derogation was permitted. The woman's submission of her case to law – not her own will – revoked her consent. She still lacked autonomy over her body and only the courts could withdraw what she was held to have conferred upon her husband: 'an irrevocable privilege to have sexual intercourse with her during such time as the ordinary relations created by such contract subsist between them' (Hawkins J in *Clarence*, 1888).

Lifelong consent to sexual intercourse in marriage was the proposition asserted by Hale, which the courts refused to challenge. The narrow list of exceptions has an absurd air, and was legalistically limited by the judiciary (Brooks, 1989) before the *R* v. *R* case (1991) rendered it redundant. In *Miller* (1954) a separation and a petition for divorce were said to be insufficient indication by a wife of her lack of desire for relations with her husband; in *Steele* (1977) starting court proceedings for a restraining order or injunction was also found to be insufficient; in *Sharples* (1990) a court order not to use or threaten violence made under s. 6 of the Domestic Proceedings and Magistrates Court Act 1978 was not enough.. The ineluctable conclusion from a review of these cases is that, as was said in *Miller*, the wife 'is in a different position from any other woman, for she has no right or power to refuse her consent.' Only the court can revoke the sexual contract on behalf of the wife; this was made clear as late as 1977 (in *Steele*). The reasoning behind this was that 'the wife, by process of law, namely, by marriage, had given consent to the husband ... but by further process of law, namely, the justices' order, her consent to marital intercourse was revoked.' This reinforced *O'Brien* (1974) where a decree nisi was said to have terminated the marriage and the wife's consent. In *Roberts* (1986) agreement between the parties, or court order or equivalent was said to be necessary. In other words, the wife's own will and intentions were not enough; she needed a piece of paper from a court.

The denial to the wife of autonomy over her body was confirmed where exceptions were elaborated. The absurdity of the general principle laid down by Hale seems to have struck neither courts nor academic commentators. For example, Professor J.C. Smith accepted 'Hale's statement, which is the foundation of the law ...' (1984: 112) while noting the exception in the *Caswell* case (1984) that it 'applies literally only to intercourse per vaginam, because he is talking about rape.' Examination of the *Caswell* case puts nonsense on stilts. The issue posed was whether the fiction of the wife's perpetual consent to intercourse extended to preliminary sexual acts. The court decided that it did, and that forced marital fellatio was not a crime. However, the husband's conduct was characterised a common assault. This absurd result was a necessary consequence of a refusal to challenge Hale's general precept.

A later case, *Kowalski* (1987), added fellatio to the list of 'exceptions' to the husband's marital right. But, again, the approach was to confirm Hale's proposition and to ignore women's humiliation and dissent. For the courts Hale's proposition required difficult distinctions between forms of activities for which consent was, or was not, required. Intercourse was distinguished from physical force in *Miller* (1954). The first was held to be implied on marriage and therefore to preclude the husband from prosecution for rape. The second gave rise to the possibility of prosecution for assault; as did fellatio after *Kowalski* (1987) and *R* v. *Henry* (1990). As Lord Keith concluded in the House of Lords: 'Those cases illustrate the contortions to which judges have found it necessary to resort because of the fiction of implied consent to sexual intercourse' (*R* v. *R* 1991).

The courts, therefore, followed a strategy of expanding the spectrum of circumstances in which the wife's implied consent was regarded as revoked. But the husband's asserted right to force himself sexually on his wife, and the wife's consequent duty to submit, with loss of personal autonomy, remained intact. As late as 1991 we find courts upholding this right (*Henry*, 1990; *R* v. *J* 1991; *R* v. *S*, 1991).

Interrogating Law: A Sacred Text Abolished?

How can we explain a lack of critical stance to Hale's statement on the part of subsequent judges? We can talk, as some feminists have done, of 'phallocentric culture'. This term is deployed to refer to the needs of the masculine imperative which receive a cultural response. As Smart (1990: 201) explains:

> The term 'phallocentrism' invokes the unconscious and raises profound questions on the part that the psyche and subjectivity play in reproducing patriarchal relations. Phallocentrism attempts to give some insight into how patriarchy is part of women's (as well as men's) unconscious, rather than a superficial system imposed from outside and kept in place by social institutions, threats or force. It attempts to address the problem of the construction of gendered identities and subjectivities. Law must, therefore, be understood both to participate in the construction of meanings and subjectivities and to do so within the terms of a phallocentric culture.

It can therefore be suggested that subsequent judges recreated the meaning attached by Hale to the relations of wife and husband.

Sexual difference is constructed in a phallocentric culture to have particular meanings. These meanings are not simply imposed. They become part of the culture itself and enter into the thinking of women and men. They acquire a taken-for-granted quality. Men also see themselves in these terms – masculinity constructs femininity but is itself constructed by the phallocentric culture. Thus Hale's statement, which fitted with other parts of English common law relating to the theory of unity of husband and wife, was accepted as part of legal culture. That the wife in such theory was to be dominated and given the status of an infant was also culturally acceptable. Nevertheless it is remarkable that such legal culture could survive into the late twentieth century when the social culture concerning gender relations appears to have undergone a gradual but profound transformation. This leads us to ask deeper questions about the judicial deference accorded to Hale's text, and why this deference eventually ceased.

Recent writing on law and its origins suggests that an explanation be sought in the notion of 'the sacred' (Goodrich, 1986; 1991). If we characterise certain ideational sources as mythical, or of divine origin, we can begin to understand the unthinking judicial acceptance of a mere proposition concocted in the seventeenth century by a single author. Not only did Hale flout the internal logic of law's system of reasoning by failing to provide authority for his proposition, but so did the inheritors of that tradition, despite the doubts expressed by a few.

In dealing with family matters it is not uncommon for courts to look to religious or sacred texts. Thus the doctrine of unity of husband and wife was frequently supported by biblical references to 'one flesh', or to 'Adams' rib' which became his wife. Even academic authors have called on the *Book of Common Prayer* to justify Hale's rationale for the marital rape exemption based on contract (Lanham, 1983: 165). Temkin provides a convincing critique of this rationale as vacuous and without foundation (1987: 45). But the continued reiteration and repetition of Hale's words in legal texts does have a mantra-like quality. East's *Pleas of the Crown* (1805, vol 1: 446) and Archbold's *Pleading and Evidence* (1822: 259) reproduced Hale's views, as did Hume's *Criminal Law of Scotland* (1797). At this point, legal texts also became sacred. We may also seek an explanation in misogyny or phallocentrism, as some writers have done in relation to Hale himself (Geis, 1977; Mitra, 1979). Various levels of explanation are possible. The query now becomes: why have Hale's sacred words been desanctified? Why has the fiction been destroyed? Why is the myth dethroned?

Examination of the reasoning of the Court of Appeal in *R* v. *R* (1991) reveals that 'commonsense' is now to be elevated to mythic status replacing the sacred texts. This is done by the Chief Justice in the phrases 'changing social attitudes', and 'what is today generally regarded as acceptable behaviour'. Recent cases in Crown Courts have also chosen this language: 'what common sense indicated ought to be the result'; 'the common law is meant to be the collective common sense of the judges' (Owen J, *R* v. *R*, 1991: 751).

In the desanctification of Hale's text various strategies are open to the judiciary. Three major paths can be identified. The first is to agree with Hale's general proposition but to elaborate further exceptions. This has been developed throughout the twentieth century and the 'exceptional' cases discussed above are examples. The second path is talk of common sense today, changing social, economic and cultural developments, and the historical context of Hale's writing. This offers to the judiciary the advantages of preserving the legitimacy of the statements of previous generations of judges. The 1991 judgments of the Court of Appeal and House of Lords, which effectively abolish the husband's marital right, fall into this category. This will be further investigated below. The final path is to recognise bodily autonomy as a general principle for women and men and to deny legitimacy to Hale's proposition and the subsequent generations of judges who upheld it in principle, even while elaborating 'exceptions'. To do this, women's perspectives from outside this law would have to be admitted.

If Hale's words have acquired the status of sacred text the question becomes: why has the marital rape exemption been removed? Formal sources of law such as the existing case law with its exceptions, and the Sexual Offences Act 1976 dealing with rape, had already been reviewed in official reports which queried whether the law was appropriate (see Law Commission, 1990, WP no 116; 1992, WP no 205). Among the informal sources can be identified: specialised pressure groups (Women Against Rape); critical academic writing (Mitra, 1979, Temkin, 1987, Brooks, 1989); articles and broadcasts in the media; public opinion. This is summed up by the Chief Justice in the Court of Appeal in the phrases 'changing social attitudes', and 'what is today generally regarded as acceptable behaviour', *R* v. *R* (1991). In the House of Lords, Lord Keith's view is that 'marriage is in modern times regarded as a partnership of equals' *R* v. *R* (1991).

Hale's proposition that 'in marriage [the wife] hath given up her body to her husband' (1736: 620) is accepted both by the House of Lords and the Court of Appeal as a correct statement of the law, albeit with exceptions. To deny Hale's statement would be to undermine the doctrine of the binding precedent system, for the legitimacy of the actions of generations of judges who upheld Hale would be questioned. But what of those subjected to the myth of the marital right? Their viewpoint on the nature of marriage, on their bodily integrity and on their autonomy of will, has been denied for two centuries.

The text of the Court of Appeal (1991) judgment categorising Hale's view as fiction can be examined at a variety of levels. It can be seen: (1) as a positivistic statement of what the law is now; (2) as legal craftwork in response to 'changing social attitudes'; (3) as a policy statement of justice to women; (4) as pre-emption of legislation proposed by the Law Commission for abolition of criminal immunity for husband-rapists (1990). Even a positive statement of what the law is requires the speaker to have a perspective on what the law was, and on what it has become. To arrive at this perspective a judge must decide what is to be excluded and what is it be authoritative. The traditional way is to confer authority on formal sources of law such as legislation and cases, and to omit other influences such as women's perspectives or policy considerations. Thus Lord Lane in the Court of Appeal (1991) refers to 'the radical solution' to the question of the marital exemption to rape, which treats Hale's proposition as based on a fiction. He presents as a drawback to this solution the provisions of a statute – the

Sexual Offenses (Amendment) Act 1976 – where rape is defined in terms of 'unlawful sexual intercourse'. The short point is that lawful sexual intercourse was said to include intercourse without a wife's consent as envisaged in the statute as interpreted by a previous court in *R* v. *J* (1991). Although this argument was later rejected by Lord Lane it is notable that discussion of a 'radical solution' was largely confined to this supposed statutory obstacle and not to principles of bodily integrity. In other words, the discussion was given over to negative propositions rather than to the assertion of positive principles of autonomy.

When the House of Lords gave judgment on the *R* v. *R* (1991) appeal the line of approach was similar to that in the Court of Appeal. What is noticeable is the effort to preserve the authority system of precedent and to maintain deference to Hale's views while at the same time abolishing the supposed immunity for marital rapists from the criminal law. The strategy adopted to achieve this is reference to another authority, the law of Scotland. Such authority, although outside the strict hierarchy of English law, can be considered relevant and persuasive. It is likely that Hume's compilation of the *Criminal Law of Scotland* (1797) which stated that a man 'cannot himself commit a rape on his own wife, who has surrendered her person to him in that sort' (1844, 4th edn., vol. 1: 306) was based on Hale. Therefore the denial of the validity of this statement in Scottish law in the *Stallard* case (1989) by the High Court of Justiciary opened the way for English law.

In *Stallard* (1989) the court expressed doubt whether Hume's statement had ever accurately expressed the law of Scotland. The judgment is notable for its scepticism about Hume's reasoning on this point. There is less deference to his book as a sacred text than was paid to Hale by English courts. The House of Lords judgment uses the more forthright judgment from Scotland to undermine Hale indirectly. This is achieved by extensive quotation, the reasoning contained therein is then said to be equally valid in English law. The legal point is simple: consent is said to be revocable, as shown by precedent cases concerning separation; separation is held not to be necessary for revocation of consent; the critical question in each case is simply whether or not consent had been withheld. This brings marital rape close to the standard definition of rape but, as Farmer (1989) points out in relation to Scottish law, the issue of implied consent remains unsettled.

Other perspectives on law, while officially omitted, are acknowledged in phrases such as 'an out-of-date rule' *R* v. *J* (1991: 765); 'as offensive a fiction as it is senseless' *R* v. *R* (1991: 749, Crown Court); 'a common law fiction which has become anachronistic and offensive' *R* v. *R* (1991: 384, Court of Appeal and House of Lords). The use of such words indicate a point of entry. No such words were used in marital rape cases prior to 1990.

The saga of the marital rape immunity is significant because it illustrates a traditional definition of marriage in which the relationship is constituted by law and not by the partners. Law still has power to define marital relations notwithstanding the recovery by wives of their legal authority over their bodies. Chapter 4 considers this further.

The story of the husband's immunity from prosecution for what is now defined as a crime has been told in terms of myths and sacred texts. This is because both law and marriage resonate with sacramental associations. I want to convey the importance of a cultural understanding of the intermingling of the legal and the matrimonial. My reasons are that later discussion in Chapters 4 and 5, particularly discussion of those excluded from marriage, is presented in cultural terms. So is the eternal appeal of marriage. For the purposes of the story of the marital rape exemption, looking to myths and to ideas of the sacred also helps us to see resistance to change in a cultural context.

Myths are not an obvious source of law but where relationships of women and men are talked of, myths inform the discourse. The classical tradition records universal themes in human lives: conception, birth, childhood, sexual union, love, betrayal, error. These find an expression in family law although their mythical origins are not acknowledged.

2
The Producers of Family Law

Where does family law come from? The classic answer is to refer the reader to general sources of law such as custom, history, common law, legislation and cases. But this answer may hide as much as it reveals. Other sources such as the myths discussed in Chapter 1 are overlooked. And surely law can be drawn from a variety of wells, including a plurality of views, a diversity of beliefs and experiences, and the popular opinions, common sense, or morals of ordinary people. The writings of academics may also play a part, which is why the presentation of law in textbooks is open to scrutiny in this respect.

We start with family law as a subject, a fairly late arrival in the academy. When books are written, or courses of learning are organised on an area of law, choices have to be made about ordering concepts, emphasis, presentation. In this the role of the academic is not dissimilar to that of the legislator. Indeed there are mutual influences and interactions. So this chapter is interested in the presentation of material and concepts in family law books in the widest sense. There has been much interest in the constitution of the family, and in the deconstruction of the unit into its component elements, but very little inquiry has gone into the construction of the academic subject. It seems that academics, while refusing to take for granted social categories, treat as natural the phenomenon of a 'subject' of study, as if it sprang ready-made into the curriculum.

Family Law as a Subject

The constitution of family law as an academic subject is fairly recent. Subjects such as contract or trusts are based on a legal construct, a concept that springs from the mind of the lawyer but that has no correspondent in the material world. Understanding contract law involves being able to define in words what a contract is. It is otherwise with family law. The subject is organised around a notion – the family – which is taken for granted, and not legally defined. It is true that courts are called upon occasionally to state whether a particular relationship satisfies the notion of family, but these judgments are made on specific legislative interpretations. No consistent or general definition has been attempted. It is assumed that, with empirical experience of families, we all know what they are. But the plurality of families is precisely the point. Pluralism fits uneasily into legal and academic discourses. Definitions of terms are central to both. This leads to suspicion of family law as an area of legal practice, and as an academic subject. Pluralism of forms opens the way for refusal of recognition of certain relationships. Yet the lack of definition of the notion of family allows a subtext of values, such as those derived from patriarchy, to control. It is in this way that law constitutes the family, both directly through forms of law-making, and indirectly through a subtext.

Traditionally family law has been concerned with questions of status: child, wife, parent, husband, legitimacy, father, cohabitant, and how these are created, altered and terminated. This is familiar stuff for lawyers, used to dealing with contracting parties, trustees, beneficiaries. Status as a large element of family law can also be understood by looking to history. Property was central to common law and its development from feudal times. The transmission of wealth depended, in part, on status-linked relationships: being an eldest son, having rights of dower as a widow. The question of status has remained central to the teaching of family law as an academic subject. Rights, duties, responsibilities, depend on the recognition of status.

Aside from the common law's interest in property, family matters concerning marriage and divorce came within the province of the ecclesiastical courts until comparatively recently. In 1857 judicial divorce was introduced, and the civil courts gradually took jurisdiction over family matters. It was somewhat later that this area of law took on an identity of its own and became a characteristic way of handling some family problems, while excluding many. As an academic subject in the undergraduate curriculum, family law achieved acceptance only in the 1960s (Wilson, 1966). It has been argued that, even today, family law is regarded in legal practice and in the hierarchy of the academy as an inferior branch of the law (O'Donovan, 1986). If this is so, the reasons are complex. We can seek them in the legal tradition already discussed, in conceptual analysis, in legal method and in the economics of legal practice.

The late arrival of family law in the legal academy means that the subject is organised around an undefined concept of family as affected by legal provisions, mainly statutes. In addition to a preoccupation with status, the subject concerns itself with welfare law, tax law, medical law, education law, and draws on knowledge from the 'psy' disciplines. Given the backgrounds of the judges, when faced with a legal problem they tend to adopt legal concepts derived from other fields of law, such as common law. Thus concepts, such as contract in relation to marital rape, or title, or possession, tend to be borrowed from other areas of law and applied in family law, even when unsuitable. For example, the Court of Appeal refused at one time to believe that Parliament had intended that a man who abused his cohabitant could be excluded from their mutual home by court order. His property rights, so important at common law, were evaluated over her right to physical security. This was overruled on appeal in *Davis* v. *Johnson* (1979).

We should also consider family law methodology. Are the methods used particular to family law, or are they the traditional common law methods? The traditional methods and concepts brought by law to the family are as follows: the establishment of the 'facts' when something has 'gone wrong'; the location of a concept to apply to the facts in a process of conversion or translation to legal terms; the allocation of responsibility, fault, blame. This type of judicial inquiry is said to be law's forte. It is not necessarily suited to family matters. Therefore a discretionary jurisdiction, sometimes referred to as 'palm-tree' or 'khadi' justice, has been developed. But this, because it involves individualised justice and not the promulgation of generalities, leads to a disrespect for family law among the legal profession.

The judiciary in the Family Division of the High Court, and in the Court of Appeal, are drawn from successful members of the bar. They do not necessarily respect or understand (in the broader sense) family law. Their contribution to the development of the subject is affected by their previous experience and training. Coming from a particular professional elite class, with a narrow social base, barristers must also work hard to be successful. As Virginia Woolf observed, this 'leaves very little time for friendship, travel or art ... That explains why most successful barristers are hardly worth sitting next [to] at dinner – they yawn so' (1938). But this must also mean a lack of broad experience of life. Although a case load which mixes crime, family, accidents, might be said to open the barrister's eyes to the darker side, two points must be remembered: first, commercial practice is the way forward to success (Naffine, 1990: Ch. 2); secondly, it is the solicitor who deals with the client, apart from a brief meeting with the barrister. So, despite appearances, the future member of the judiciary is drawn from a priestly cast 'professionally cocooned in his chambers and at court from the realities of non-legal life' (Pannick, 1987: 53). As Pannick concludes:

> It is, then, not surprising that a Bench composed almost entirely of former barristers should lack expertise and knowledge of many of the matters which are central to the lives of those people who come into court as litigants or witnesses. Nor is it surprising that a Bench so composed should display a fairly uniform set of social values or should have a homogeneous independent school and Oxbridge educational background.

If family law is incoherent or contradictory, why does this create a lack of respect on the part of legal professionals? The expectation of coherence may be a product of a form of legal education, with a positivist bias, which assumes that a set of principles and rules can be organised and distilled from legal material, and then applied to problems. In other words, the critique of family law may be the product of a narrow and limited conception of law, in which the lawyer's task is to state what the law 'is'. Such an approach is difficult in family law where the messiness of people's lives will keep intruding into law's desire for dispassionate neutrality. There is an immediacy about issues of, for example, surrogate motherhood, sexual abuse, issues which are difficult to mask in legal language. The values that are chosen in the regulation of these issues are evident. Again, this puts the judge on the spot. Although he may claim to be an objective, impartial interpreter, who merely declares what the law 'is', public criticism can enter in. This is because, despite what was said above about the utilisation of existing legal concepts, family law is not easily reduced to the technical.

The Judges

Who are the judges? As one of the most important sources of formal family law, both as creators and interpreters, what special skills do the judiciary have? Lord Lane in *R* v. *R* (1991, CA) admitted the flexibility of the common law which can change. Lord Keith in *R* v. *R* (1991, HL) talked of a legal capacity for evolution. Such change draws on informal sources of law. How well-equipped are judges in recognising these? The Family Division of the High Court has a special role in the creation and interpretation of family law. It is the appellate court for cases from family courts at Magistrates' and County level; it has first instance jurisdiction for contested divorces and custody cases; it sets the policy in family matters. Examining where its judges come from gives a fair picture of the creators of family law.

The Family Division has a president, Sir Stephen Brown, and 17 members, of whom two are women. There is also a woman member of the Court of Appeal, Lord Justice Butler-Sloss, who is often called upon in family cases, presumably because women are assumed to be experienced in such matters. Few of the members of the Family Division have practised in the area. Most have come from commercial or chancery practices. For example, a recent obituary of Sir Alan Orr documents his appointment in 1965 to the High Court which 'somewhat strangely sent him to the then Probate Divorce and Admiralty Division to do divorce work of which he had virtually no experience' (*Independent*, 12 April 1991). Too often, at the bar, such an appointment to the Family Division is seen as a punishment. Details of the ages, background, and experience of the 18 members of the Family Division reveal the following: eleven were born in the 1930s;

the others earlier. All have a background of practice at the bar. Of the 18, only four do not have an educational background that includes Oxford or Cambridge. Among these four are the two women members. Seven have previous experience of family law, very often as chair of the Family Law Bar Association, but most do not. None of this is surprising. It conforms to studies of the judiciary and career patterns at the bar. It does, however, raise questions about the understanding and knowledge that is brought to bear on the production of family law, particularly given the common law's capacity for evolution 'in the light of changing social, economic and cultural developments' *R* v. *R*, 1991, HL).

Other Family Law Sources

The formal sources of law, other than cases, are legislation and custom. The former is first in the hierarchy. For example, in 1990 the Law Commission produced a working paper proposing abolition of, or curtailment of, the male marital right. Considerable reference is made in that document to the law elsewhere, both legislative and judicial. For example, the highest courts in Scotland and Israel have denied that the marital rape exemption forms part of their law. In other jurisdictions, such as Victoria, New South Wales, Western Australia, Queensland, Tasmania, Canada, New Zealand, Nebraska, Florida and New Jersey, legislation has been enacted to abolish the exemption. This is the approach advocated by the Law Commission and by certain members of the judiciary (e.g. Rougier J in *R* v. *J* (1991)). There is, of course, a distinction between saying that a law is a fiction and can therefore be declared to form no part of English law, and saying that a law, fictitious as it may be, is so well rooted as to require legislation for its extraction.

According to internal legal logic, legislation is superior to other forms of law. Much of family law is derived from this source, often after the publication of consultation documents by government departments or by the Law Commission. But a broad approach to family law must look beyond formal sources. Legal personnel such as practitioners, registrars, court welfare officers, clerks to the magistrates, have an active part in the process whereby law is interpreted and applied. This is so also for adoption social workers, child-care officers, and many others charged by the state with administering families.

It is important to understand the hierarchy of family laws in which legislation is the major and superior source. But there is a context to the operation of the law. Procedures and processes involving legal and state personnel of various kinds and at various levels must also be studied if we are to understand fully the nature of family law. These matters are often omitted from textbooks.

Students of family law are faced with an array of legislation, cases, rules and procedures. Textbooks help to make sense of this by organising the material and concepts, such as marriage or child-custody disputes. General principles, such as the welfare of the child, are used at both a normative and an explanatory level. But students and teachers must ask themselves what is omitted in this, and whether this affects how family law is perceived and practised. The influence of textbook writers, and of theorists, on the presentation and perception of family law is significant. The next section considers this in the light of general reflections on legal education.

The Role of Legal Education in the Production of Family Law

The following comments on the education of lawyers in the common law tradition are not intended as a general theory or account. Rather, the object is to point to certain features, a *mentalite*, which define both professional and academic training. The point being made is that the production of family law in practice and in the academy is influenced by the *mentalite* under discussion (Collier, 1991a). The history of legal education in the common law world is marked by three aspects: the late arrival of law as an academic subject in universities; training for law as a practical profession, rather than as a liberal discipline; social homogeneity among legal practitioners, and the inculcation of these values among future lawyers.

The dominant tradition in England has been of the legal profession training its future members. Although certain examinations have been required for entry, great emphasis has been placed on pupillage at the bar and practical training (articles) for solicitors. As a discipline within the academy, law has not been accorded the facilities or respect given to other subjects. According to Sugarman's historical study (1986) the law academics of the nineteenth and early twentieth century tried to find a place between the profession and the academy. The result – a style of legal teaching that was narrow, expository and practice oriented – involved deference to an older trade-school tradition.

There has been a movement away from this tradition in the late twentieth century, and it is fair to say that teachers of family law have been sensitive to empirical studies, policy arguments and inter-disciplinary work generally. But earlier traditions continue to exercise an influence. Thus, as Sugarman points out, legal educators attempt to present law as 'essentially a simple, unified, coherent whole' (Sugarman, 1986: 34). This presentation of law as a science 'ultimately governed by principles akin to the laws of natural sciences and ... a subject worthy of a place in the university firmament' (Sugarman, 1986: 30) was designed to avoid trespassing on the territory of the profession and to claim a place in the academy. But this was a highly abstract 'science' of legal principles that avoided both theory and empiricism.

The textbooks that emerged from this presentation of law as a science contained sets of legal principles and rules that could be learned and applied to problems. Learning the law for students became learning the principles identified by legal educators. The result, according to Sugarman (1986: 51), is 'the teaching of law as a simple set of rules; that examinations test the ability to resolve legal problems by reference to certain "pat" answers; and that law texts and teaching are "vocational" (albeit in a peculiarly narrow and artificial sense) and examination-oriented' (1986: 51). Mary Jane Mossman (1986) argues that legal method is impervious to fundamental questioning about its process.

This tradition has been subjected to a healthy critique. To Duncan Kennedy, American legal education is 'training for hierarchy' (Kennedy, 1982). In Australia, Thornton (1986; 1989) has found a 'narrow, doctrinal, atheoretical' style of legal teaching: 'There is little understanding of the study of law as an interdisciplinary, contextual and critical exercise' (Thornton, 1986: 22). Bankowski and Mungham (1976: 82) describe English legal education as 'ahistorical, pedestrian and encouraging only a narrow cognitive sense of law'.

Deference to the legal profession has characterised the approach of legal academics to their subject. Many reasons can be suggested for this, including the late arrival of law to the academy, the role of the judiciary as interpreters of the law, the socialisation of the educators themselves. This final point is the focus of what follows. Studies of the legal profession in the common law world reveal the homogeneity of its members. Discussions of the social groups from which lawyers are drawn inevitably focus on gender, race and class. Atiyah (1983: 11) gives us some simple statistics on the composition of the English bench. Nearly all judges are white, middle-aged or elderly men, as earlier details of the membership of the Family Division of the High Court confirm. Few members of the judicial committee of the House of Lords, the highest court, or of the Court of Appeal, are under 60. They are drawn almost exclusively from the professional and managerial classes, have been privately educated and subsequently studied at Oxbridge in the majority. As Pannick (1987: 59) sums it up: 'The English judiciary includes few women, even fewer blacks, and nobody under the age of 40 ... It is disturbing that our judges come from so narrow a range of the community.'

Changes in the composition of the bench and the legal profession are in process. Senior solicitors, including the president of the Law Society, have urged the Lord Chancellor to appoint more non-white men and women, and more women generally, to the bench. It is also suggested that solicitors, in daily contact with clients, have skills and knowledge appropriate for membership of the judiciary (*New Law Journal*, 1991: 1097). The Lord Chancellor has taken counsel's opinion (advice from a barrister) to the effect that the under-representation of women and ethnic minorities in judicial appointments is not indirect discrimination under the Sex Discrimination Act 1975 and the Race Relations Act 1976. In a letter to the President of the Law Society (*New Law Journal*, 1991: 1062), he asserts:

> I will succeed in my objective of increasing the number of women on the Bench only if I can find a suitable proportion of women in the practising profession of the appropriate age and standing. At present the pool of female candidates, both barristers and solicitors, is a very small proportion of the total ... a similar problem exists with members of the ethnic minorities.

The discretion exercised by the judiciary in choosing facts, law, sentences and awarding costs is significant power. In a just society the choice of such powerful persons must be justified. Pannick (1987: 59) argues that diverse backgrounds, ages, races and sexes among the judiciary are necessary because 'it is inequitable in a democratic society that one set of values should predominate' and because of the danger that the unrepresented 'will lose respect for the law'. The latter objection is pragmatic but the former is substantial. What it overlooks, however, is that the clubability of the bar affects not only values, but ways of seeing. A wider group of disparate backgrounds may be inculcated into a narrow mentality through membership of an elite group. At present, success as a legal practitioner, creating eligibility for judicial appointments, depends on the acceptance of dominant values and perspectives.

The attitudes inculcated by membership of the legal profession are 'not simply a function of social homogeneity: the fact that at the senior levels of the profession we find like types working closely together in a tightly knit social world' (Naffine, 1990: 89). What Naffine and others suggest is that legal practice largely involves the privileged advising the privileged, in areas of business, commerce, tax, trusts, competition law. Lawyers who practice in the family law area are largely outside this golden circle. As will be shown later, legal aid is very important to the family law practitioner as it enables advice to, and representation of, disadvantaged clients. It may even be that such practitioners develop a subculture within the legal profession. Nevertheless, the general point is that there is a community of outlook among lawyers that has influenced the academic presentation of the law in textbooks and elsewhere.

It is not self-evident that writers on family law will reflect the views of powerful judges and lawyers about their subject. What is being suggested here is that the reader be alert to the possibility of such uncritical acceptance. According to the realist schools of jurisprudence, law is what the courts say and do (Frank, 1949). If that is so, this places power with those defined as members of courts. However, writers on family law come from a wide spectrum of theoretical perspectives, as will be seen in the next section. The classic textbooks present the law 'as it is'.

Telling Stories about Family and Law

This section considers a variety of methods of thinking and writing about family and law. It illustrates the overlap between methods, theories and writing styles. It is not being claimed that there is one way or a 'right' way. On the contrary, the discussion below shows how different methods, theories and presentations can reveal various parts of the picture. The point is to lead the reader to query other texts which do not discuss these various options. At the same time the reader should bear in mind the power of the present writer to choose, define, include and omit. There is a hierarchy of family law texts; those giving an account of what the law 'is' perform the traditional task of the legal textbook. A book such as this, of critical commentary, is considered marginal.

Positivism
In legal discourse positivism is taken to be an assertion of what the law is. This is the dominant school in English jurisprudence. Law is a self-referential system of rules that derives its authority from law. In this tradition sources of law are not only formal but within a hierarchy. Cases refer back to earlier, precedent cases. Statutes have a stronger authority than cases. Excluded are broader questions of law's provenance in non-formal legal sources, alternative ways of seeing and doing.

In the social sciences the term 'positivism' refers to a way of interpreting people's experience of social life which insists that material and social worlds are essentially the same. Facts of various kinds are assumed to exist, which can be discovered or uncovered by the collecting of evidence. This is presented as a scientific approach (Stanley and Wise, 1983: Ch. 1). In relation to divorce, some doubt has been expressed by the Law Commission as to whether such a scientific approach to human relationships is possible. The traditional legal approach is to establish the facts as one true set of events, discoverable by reference to witnesses, material evidence, interpreted by technical evidence in which responsibility and blame are allocated with reference to the evidence. Whether such a method is appropriate to the termination of marriage is now a major question (Law Commission, 1990, no 192). Similar questions are being asked about child abuse. But even if we eventually conclude that positivism is unsuited to family law, there remains a broader question of its suitability as a legal method.

Positivism is not confined to method. It is also a way of seeing the world, a theory through which to view and present events and people, including oneself. The virtue of this approach for law is that lawyers are in control, with the power of definition and exclusion. Rules of procedure and evidence are used to shape acceptable facts and to omit alternative perspectives and claims. Critics of positivism point to a denial of a voice to the powerless, to minorities, to those who are 'different'. Since law's authority comes only from law, transcendental notions of human rights cannot enter in. Power remains with the powerful.

Positivist methodology in social science traditionally treated the family as an entity, a concept that was not questioned. More recently feminist theory has questioned this 'black box' theory of the family and has opened up the family unit and unpacked the box. Whereas family members were assumed to have shared values and common goals, pluralism has been shown to exist within the family. The assumed identity of interests has been exploded as family members are revealed to have their own standpoint. Instead of being taken for granted as unit and united, the family has been politicised and problematised. Among responses are child-centred theories, feminist analyses, father-centred work around the family. As fictions are exposed, other myths are revealed. For example, the fiction of wife and husband as unit informed another fiction, that of a wife's perpetual consent to sexual inter-course.

Functionalism
Studying what an institution does, or is assumed to do, is the task of the functionalist. Writers on family law, dissatisfied with positivistic statements of what the law is, have broadened their approach by becoming functionalists. Leading examples have come from John Eekelaar (1978; 1984), who identifies three major tasks for family law: to protect, to adjust and to support. The protective function requires the law to protect family members from detriment: physical, emotional and economic. The adjustive function requires the law to help people whose family unit is in difficulty to adjust to their new situation. The supportive function is concerned not only with the welfare of individual family members but also with the continued stability of the family as a whole.

Looking to law's goals, rather than stating what the law is, has aided definition and clarity in discussion of family law. In addition, clear goals for the law enable assessment of its success or failure, of whether change in formal sources is needed. Informal sources of law may be able to enter in through a functionalist discourse, particularly in assessment.

Critics of functionalism argue that definition and clarity are not entirely achieved. Formal sources of law are not always internally consistent; different pieces of legislation send different messages because of conflicting aims. In other words, goals are not always coherent or consistent. This is particularly so in a non-codified legal system such as that of England and Wales. Dewar points to the following criticisms: (a) the functions of institutions are rarely obvious and verification or falsification of what a particular institution stands for is not possible; (b) the concept of protection and the measurement of its success lack clarity; (c) in the relationship between perceived function and institution it is unclear whether a particular institution only can perform the function (Dewar, 1989: 3).

The above criticisms are internal, that is, they merely point to the incoherence of functionalism. A deeper problem is that functionalism does not question the allocation of power within the family. To some extent the family continues to be treated as a 'black box' into which the law does not peer until it starts to collapse. Law undoubtedly has a role when things go wrong in the family, and that this purpose has been clarified extensively. But over-concentration on this aspect of law's role may obscure the constitution of gender, parent–child and marital relationships through the messages sent by law. This constitutive element of law may itself lead to the pathological, 'gone-wrong', function identified for law (O'Donovan, 1979). For example, whereas law purports to protect members of families from violence, it may also facilitate that violence through its allocation of authority to husbands or parents. Through its definitions and allocation of status, law constructs the meaning of 'wife' or 'child'. The functional family has its opposite in the 'dysfunctional family'. This concept, beloved of family theorists and state agents such as social workers, implies the existence of an ideal family. But what is that? A family that subordinates its vulnerable members? The question *cui bono?* applies again.

Functionalism has been criticised as too narrow an approach, one that limits the range of inquiry. As a moral theory it is sexist in its beliefs and assumptions. Social stability is emphasised, with rules and norms internalised, and women's role defined in certain terms; and when women broke out this was labelled 'dysfunctional'. There can be little doubt that feminist research has opened up new questions which could not be asked under a functionalist methodology. These concern power within the family, the privileging of family members on the basis of gender by state agencies, the silence of the subordinated (MacKinnon, 1987). Postmodern theory emphasises the regulatory aspect of mechanisms outside law, such as medical and administrative apparata, and agents such as child-care officers, educators, medical personnel, social workers (Foucault, 1979, 1981; Donzelot, 1979). We should, however, be wary of setting definitions of functionalists in concrete: there is evidence that those who adopt a goal-oriented analysis of law are aware of law's symbolic functions. They may also be influenced by other approaches to the analysis of law.

Familialism

Building on insights of Foucault and Donzelot who identified a complex web of mechanisms in which power is diffused, some writers advocate familialism as a way of seeing families and law. The term originates in Donzelot's book *The Policing of Families* (1979) and refers to ideologies modelled on family values – or values taken to be associated with families. It is said that other aspects of life are presented in terms of these values. Examples abound in advertising, television programmes and political rhetoric. Familialism should be taken as a term criticising these social developments, and the consequent idealisation of the family. However, there is also an explanatory level, in that the criticism is based on interpretations of history. Thus familialism purports to explain in historical, economic and social terms the spread of family ideology.

According to Donzelot's broad review, in which periodisation is largely unspecified, recent family history is as follows:

> Once upon a time there was the family of the Ancien Regime where patriarchal authority reigned, and family members were protected from other established power. Because of changes within and without families lost their autonomy. Although the bourgeois family and the working class family were differently affected, the family came under the supervision of various experts, such as psychiatrists, psychologists, doctors, health visitors, social workers, educators. This came about because of collaboration between the mother of the bourgeois family and the hygiene specialists. Instead of living happily ever after the family was weakened. The realm of the social was developed 'in relation to which the family is both queen and prisoner'. (Donzelot, 1979: 7)

As the summary above suggests, there is a mythological aspect to this story. Caution should be exercised when reference is made to familialism for the following reasons: first there is an element of myth, as suggested above; second, the notion of family, as deployed by Donzelot, is an essentialist notion. He seems to have some quintessential, or even stereotypical family in mind; third, Donzelot idealizes the authoritarian, patriarchal family, but describes his modern family as pathological; fourth, there is an incipient anti-feminism in Donzelot's thesis of blaming the perceived ills of the family on women; fifth, subsequent texts give a variety of meanings to familialism, for example Dewar ascribes familialism to a new strand of feminist thinking about law which looks to effects rather than goals (Dewar, 1989: 6). It is proposed that a consequentialist perspective will reveal the conditions under which patriarchal relations survive.

The creation of myths about some former family is useful as an exercise of contrast with and critique of the present. But the idealisation of the past or of the present should make us wary. Which families in the lost world of the past are to be preferred to which families of the present? Are we talking of material comfort, economic security, patriarchal authority, intervention by regulators, sexuality, personal freedom, love? The essentialist nature of 'golden age of the family' accounts must give rise to scepticism (see also Lasch (1977) for another example).

Familialism, as a critical term, analyses a discourse that is said to operate in civil and public society. That advertising, the popular press, and the media in general depict a certain family form as the norm is no doubt true. The idealisation of the 'cornflakes family' has already been discussed. No doubt, also, its existence is largely a myth. But the point goes further, pointing to an emphasis on family and personal lives rather than public lives. This is summed up in the phrase 'the commercialization of sex and the sexualization of commerce'. The late twentieth century has seen a growth in the information trade and in the commodification of sex. Bring these two elements together and the outcome is evident.

Those critics who have developed the notion of familialism have various goals. First, there are those who idealise the past. The family of the past may be that of the *ancien régime*, or of the medieval peasantry, or of the nineteenth-century bourgeoisie. Second, some critics wish to maintain an analysis that has had purchase in this century: the old Marxian functionalism that took the bourgeois family as object of criticism. Third, others want to enlist sympathy for the working-class family as subject to surveillance by experts. Fourth, some have an idealised view of human nature and believe that if the family did not exist, love, trust and nurturance would be given and received within society as a whole. Thus Barrett and McIntosh: 'It is as if the family has drawn comfort and security into itself and left the outside world bereft. As a bastion against a bleak society it has made that society bleak' (1982: 80).

In summary, three disparate aspects emerge from the writing that deploys the concept of familialism. From Foucault and Donzelot we receive the important insight that power is not only juridical, but that in regulating the family the 'psy' experts are pervasive. Unfortunately, the feminist analysis of male power is ignored. From Barrett and McIntosh comes a warning that the family is anti-social in that it pulls people away from participation in the life of society in general, thus impoverishing worlds outside the home. From the 'feminist familialists' comes the emphasis on effects: 'By taking women rather than law as the starting point, it can be seen that the effect ... of law is the promotion of a particular family form'(Dewar, 1989: 6). But this is not a novel point, since this insight pre-dates the critique of familialism (O'Donovan, 1979). The category 'women' is here so unspecific as to be almost meaningless. Furthermore, it is not evident that a concentration on 'effect' gets away from functionalism despite the claim that familialism ignores intentions and goals. Brophy and Smart have suggested that analysis of effects will reveal the material and ideological conditions under which patriarchal relations survive, and that law's active role is in the reproduction of these (Smart, 1984: Ch. 1; Brophy and Smart, 1985; Brophy, 1985). But is this a conscious or unconscious goal/effect of law?

Familialism may open up more questions than functionalism. Where the former is said to look to effects the latter is said to look to intentions. But surely research on families and law must do both? There are examples of empirical research which examine whether what happens is what was intended (Davis and Murch on divorce, 1988; Dingwall, Eekelaar and Murray on children 1983). Perhaps the distinction lies with the starting place. Functionalists accept what is officially said to be the purpose or goal of a particular piece of legislation, such as 'to buttress the stability of marriage' or 'to protect children'. The research attempts to establish whether this occurs. Feminist familialists start by asking about laws' effects on women and move from there to the advantages given to certain family forms. Functionalism privileges official intentions and views; familialism privileges women over children, opening up the criticism that family members do not share the identity of interests so often assumed by law and policy (Pahl, 1989).

The importance given to law in these explanatory theories may be queried. It is not possible to provide an over-arching or essentialist theory of the relationship between families and law; nor is it possible to declare that law reinforces one particular family form. As we shall see throughout this book, the relationship is dynamic. Where some aspects of family law are going through a stage of legal withdrawal, such as divorce, others are in the throes of judicialisation, under the Children Act 1989.

The Public/Private Split
Understanding of family and law may be aided by a form of analysis which focuses on the distinction between the public and the private (Olsen, 1983; O'Donovan, 1985; Naffine, 1990). These terms refer to two distinct social realms constituted within liberal social philosophy divided from one another by legal regulation. The public realm is presented as that of state, market and politics, and is the world of men; the private realm, associated primarily with women, is the world of family. The values prevalent in the former are those of individualism; in the latter self-sacrifice and altruism are idealised. This picture of a

dichotomised world contains a scene in which subordinated family members lack legal power. Law's respect for the privacy of the family leaves women and children unequal to men. Male power is not only derived from structures external to the family, from the public world, but it is reinforced by ideologies of family privacy, and exercised within the family. But this is only one sense in which the distinction is made.

The notion of 'public' or 'private' makes sense only as one element in a paired opposition. As Weintraub (1990: 2) points out, we need to know with what it is being contrasted (explicitly or implicitly) and on what basis the contrast is being drawn. This clarification is important, as the public/private distinction has been used in social scientific work other than law (Elshtain, 1981; Goffman, 1971; Habermas, 1989; Pateman, 1988). If we take the contrast as distinguishing different kinds of human action and different realms of social life, then four major uses of the distinction can be analysed.

Weintraub (1990: 4) identifies first the liberal-economist model, which sees the private/public distinction in terms of a contrast between state administration and the market economy. The second contrast is between the 'public' realms of politics, distinct from both market and state. The third contrast is that drawn by Aries (1962;1977;1987–1990) and others, which presents the 'public' as the social sphere. Finally, in feminist analyses, the 'private' is the realm of family, intimacy and domesticity. State, market and, indeed, the political, tend to be grouped together as the undifferentiated 'public'.

Critics of feminist public/private analyses argue that the discussion concentrates exclusively on law and overlooks other forms of regulation of the family. The reference is to procedures and practices of social workers, of health-care professionals, of public health officers, or educators, of all those for whom the family is a site of intervention, or who promote a particular family form. But this criticism would be infinitely expanded through reference to other influences on family relationships: gender role socialisation, child-raising practices, ideologies purveyed by schools, media presentations including advertising, novels, films – the danger is that the major point will be lost in a welter of examples and counter examples. Focus on law does not preclude recognition of other influences on the family. Law, however, is an important signifier of power. Law also claims the power of definition and translation: all human action and discourse may be defined and translated into legal terms prior to legal regulation. The degree to which other procedures and practices regulate may be questioned.

More telling is the short point that the family exists in the public realm as a means of government, that is, the state uses the family as an ally: 'the family appeared as a positive solution to the problems of the regulation of morality, health and procreation posed by a liberal definition of the limits of legitimate state action' (Rose, 1987: 70). Unfortunately this point is itself open to the criticism that it treats the family in a functionalist way as a 'black box'.

Critical Family Law

Some writers suggest that analysis of the public/private split and familialism are part of a larger movement known as critical family law. The main tenets of the critical movement may be identified as follows: rejection of formalism and of law's objectivity; assertion that law is political and is mixed in the totality of social relations and institutions; those elements in law which constitute and define the social world with which it intersects.

Freeman expresses the view that 'at the root of a critical theory of family law is the public/private dichotomy' (1985: 174). Critical method proceeds by identifying a fundamental contradiction running through the legal and social structure. In the case of family law it is between the values of individualism and the values of altruism, but it may be characterised as between individual freedom and community. Such contradictions lead to incoherence. The interpenetration of the social and legal is a totality in which it is impossible to decipher which is determinative.

The objection has been made that in liberal society various values abound, including those of family and market. Eekelaar argues that it is a paradox, but not a contradiction, that restraint has to be exercised so that freedom may be enjoyed; that choice is conflict but not contradiction; that a single over-arching dichotomy of 'public and private' is suspect when confronting categories such as market, state and civil society; that clear-cut differences between family values and commercial values are problematic (Eekelaar, 1989: 251–4). This is supported by the argument that the family can be described in terms of public values as follows: 'the strength of legal involvement in enforcement of family solidarity is directly related to the extent to which the family system is failing to fulfil its role as resource distributor within the community' (Eekelaar, 1989: 255). In other words, the family is assumed to operate efficiently, and law comes in only when things go wrong.

Eekelaar's response to critical family law is to reassert law's role as a public instrument. Where the public interest is threatened by the 'breakdown of family life' (1989: 255) then law or regulatory practices entered in. Eekelaar retains an instrumental approach: 'The functioning of what is socially defined as private may often be a matter of public interest' (1989: 258). Despite the empiricism of his general approach he does not ask the following kinds of question. Is family life healthy where subordinate members are silent? Can law protect against violences of which it knows nothing? Is there a public interest in individual human rights? How is the public interest defined? Is it confined to the pockets of the taxpayer? According to Eekelaar it is law's role to translate policy choices between conflicting values into solutions within a coherent framework. Part of the law's job is to ensure that 'the legal result is not in itself self-contradictory or incoherent'. It is this which maintains the relative autonomy of law from the social forces it expresses (1989: 20). The job of translation is an indication of law's power. That power is at the heart of this discussion of different ways of presenting family and law.

A Postmodernistic Approach to Family Law?

As can be deduced from the preceding discussion, each form of theorisation of family law has its drawbacks and critics. Even positivism, which claims to state what the law is, as opposed to theorising about it, has been exposed as an inadequate theory, or way of presenting law. Perhaps the difficulty with the approaches outlined above is that they attempt too much. In recent years legal writers, drawing on the work of literary critics, architects, writers of fiction and others concerned with aesthetics, have proposed postmodern jurisprudence. This is an approach to law which is against large-scale theories, preferring small-scale and open accounts of experiences of the world. It involves a rejection of the idea that a full and perfect theory will one day be discovered that can explain the nature of law. It emphasises form and style as well as content.

Another way of presenting this provisional character of legal theory is that of Lee (1990) who makes an analogy between writing about law and Monet's 30 studies of the Cathedral at Rouen:

> Each analysis of law gives us one view of the cathedral of law. It can do no more. It cannot paint the cathedral of law from all angles. At different times, the view from the same place is different. Each picture tells us something about the cathedral but also something about the painter and his or her vantage points ... what we need is to paint the picture of law from all manner of perspectives and from inside the cathedral. (Lee, 1990)

Postmodernism gives attention to the stories of the excluded, the oppressed; stories that have been ignored or repressed. Just as feminist theory led to the recovery and uncovering of the pasts of women, so other stories can now emerge. The married woman at common law was feme covert, whose existence was covered by her husband's legal personality. She has gradually been uncovered, although as we saw in the discussion of marital rape, this has taken considerable time. The existences of children are covered by the legal powers of their parents. The work of recovery and uncovering of childhood experiences has only just begun.

What postmodernism proposes is various realities, various stories, various standpoints. For law this is a problem. Legal method is positivistic. It assumes that facts exist which can be discovered or uncovered through collection. The rules of evidence are then applied to these facts to reduce them to 'material facts'. Legal rules are then identified and applied. There may be certain social events to which this method can be applied, for example a road accident, in which responsibility is to be allocated. But if we compare a road accident in which a child is hurt with a case of suspected child abuse, methodological difficulties emerge. As Carty and Mair (1990) document, uncovering facts, or 'the truth' about childhood experiences is not always possible. As adults argue about methods and truth, the child may be forgotten.

Divorce is another area of family law in which traditional legal methods of uncovering truth and responsibility are inapplicable. The allocation of blame for the breakdown of marriage may not be possible or fruitful, particularly where children are involved. For law, which has one goal of stigmatising cruel behaviour such as violence, but has another goal of giving a decent burial to dead marriages, finding the appropriate method is difficult.

Autopoietic Theory

A radical alteration of the way questions about norms and facts are posed has come from the general theory of self-referential autopoietic systems. Originating with Niklas Luhmann (1983, 1984), the theory concerns a system that produces and reproduces its own elements by the interaction of its elements. As Luhmann (1989, 137) explains: 'One can conceive of law as a social system only if one takes into consideration the fact that this system is a subsystem as well.' In this theory law and society are not separated, but rather law is a 'differentiated functional system within society'. The legal system continually engages in 'the self-reproduction (autopoiesis) of the overall social system', and thus 'participates in society's construction of reality' (Luhman, 1989: 138).

Drawing on the term 'discourse' developed by Foucault, Gunther Teubner (1987a) argues that legal discourse is autopoietic. In this theoretical model law exists quite independently of the individuals who operate the system. Legal discourse is one form of communication that constructs social reality. Social organisations 'think', that is create their own forms of knowledge, independently of people involved in the system. This departs from critical studies of the law in that individual actors, such as judges, are presented as products of an autopoietic system rather than as players. 'According to this view, therefore, little would be changed by selecting and training judges differently or by replacing them with those more sympathetic to, say, feminist or anti-racist causes' (King, 1991: 3).

Those involved in legal communications, according to Teubner (1988: 133) became 'role-bundles, character masks, internal products of legal communications' existing only as constructs, but not human actors. Thus legal concepts such as the 'reasonable man' or the 'welfare of the child' do not refer to real people but to constructs. But law does come up against people and 'knowledge' produced in other discourses such as those concerning economics, psychology, social work. When this happens, despite appearances, there is only 'interference' as the gap between the separate discourses of knowledge cannot be bridged. Attempts to communicate across the divide result in confused thinking and decision-making. The theory is a critique of law's inability to deal with disputes.

This theory must pose problems for the family lawyer who hopes to discuss family therapy, or predictions about a child's future adjustment or development with the 'psy' specialists. In an application of the theory to law's thinking about children, King and Piper (1991) argue that law cannot immunise itself from realities produced by other discourses. But they find that the child welfare discourse is enslaved by law and that the real child becomes a 'semantic artifact' constructed by legal discourse. So the problem is this: on the one hand law is 'closed' to knowledge produced by other discourses; on the other hand, because of welfarist concerns for children, law must recognise other 'reality discourses'. Law is therefore in an 'epistemic trap', that is, it needs to open up but it cannot. The solution for Teubner is that law must become 'reflexive', that is partially to renounce its authority by providing the 'norms of procedure, organisation and competencies that aid other social systems' (King and Piper, 1991: 31).

King and Piper use autopoietic theory to explain certain aspects of family law. To do so they construct a model of law as adversarial, involving a reconstruction of past behaviours as a basis for presenting decisions, moralistic, evidence-centred, and polarising (King and Piper, 1991: 81–83). But some may see this model as more appropriate to law's method of dealing with motor accidents than with family law which has developed a discretionary, therapeutic mode, particularly in relation to disputes over children. While King and Piper's conclusion that law and its procedures are harmful to children may be accurate, the original source of the harm is correctly identified as parental lack or conflict. The specific criticisms of law made by the authors are that law simplifies by reducing the social world to manageable concepts; that law individualises; that law excludes versions of reality it is unable to handle; that law is adversarial; that law compartmentalises; and that law enslaves child welfare science. They find the answer to the specific problems they raise in the 'child responsiveness' of French law, in which intervention by the *juge des enfants* is continuous rather than episodic.

It is not evident that King and Piper need to turn to autopoietic theory in order to make the criticisms of English law that they do, or that the French system of handling cases concerning children might not be subjected to a similar autopoietic analysis by another theorist. A major doubt must also centre on autopoiesis itself. Luhmann (1989) sees certainty and the stabilising of expectations and behaviour in a world without consensus or moral absolutes as major tasks of law. If this is correct, then the relative content of law does not appear important. Law can be explained through systems theory. It derives its legitimacy from reference back to its organisational structure and tasks, and not from its interaction with other areas of knowledge such as psychology. At this point the theory comes close to positivism despite the critique of law contained within it.

This Text

The reader may be curious as to the theory espoused by this text. Is it positivistic? Does the writer remain committed to her earlier explanations about the public/private divide? Are we all postmodernists?

As this text proposes to open up questions and meanings to the reader, no one theory is advanced. Rather, the style of writing of chapters is influenced by the material. Whereas this chapter has been written in expository style in order to map and provide signposts, other chapters, such as those on marriage, divorce and children merit different presentations. Although this may appear an eclectic fashion of presenting material and arguments, the writer hopes that the effect will be a broadening and enriching of the classic methods of discussing family law. It is also hoped that the idea of different experiences of, and viewpoints on, law will be illustrated. An example from the marital rape saga is appropriate as that chapter is closed. In 1980 the proposal to criminalise marital rape was rejected with these official words:

> The type of questions which investigating police offers would have to ask would be greatly resented by husbands and families. The family ties would be severed and the wife with children would have to cope with her emotional, social and financial problems as best she could; and possibly the children might resent what she had done to their father. (Criminal Law Revision Committee, 1980: para 33)

The reinforcing of the viewpoint of power is evident.

3
Family Forms

What stories do we human beings tell ourselves about families? In making sense of ourselves and our world, families are of immediate significance to us. These are the places in which most of us are socialised; where we learn that boys are different from girls; where mothers take care of the physical and the emotional, while fathers earn the money.

We accept as natural social arrangements in which the sexes are opposed. Even if our own lives do not conform to the traditional family story, we know and understand all about it. The myth, the ideal, and the reality of the family story is what this chapter is about.

The organising concepts of family law such as marriage or child protection are universal in stories across time and space. It can be argued that these already exist as social phenomena or as relationships before becoming intermingled with law. By this is meant that stories of family or group, with children dependent on mothers, pre-date stories of law. The purpose here is not to enter into this debate, but to stress law's role in constituting a particular family form, which is now perceived as natural. This is a reference to the nuclear family, headed by the husband and father. It is often said that law privileges particular forms and particular members of families. What is meant by this is that legislative and social policies encourage and reinforce certain relationships, such as marriage; despite egalitarian measures, the male remains pre-eminent as household head, and families without such a head are considered a problem.

Varying and Various Forms of Families

The idealised family, often known as the 'cornflakes' family, has been much derided in critical writing. It is pointed out that: the average family of mother, father, and 1.8 children is the product of statistics and not of life; households containing dependent children are exceptional; of those households containing children, 12 per cent are single-parented; more than a quarter of all children are born outside marriage, the majority to stable cohabiting couples; 10 per cent of households contain adults living alone (Central Statistics Office, 1991: Ch. 2). This chapter is interested in the extent to which law upholds the idealised family, which may never have existed but which is represented in advertising and fiction. If it did exist, this was for only a brief period in the mid twentieth century.

The image of the ideal family, with father at work outside the home supporting a dependent wife and children in a middle-class lifestyle, has had a considerable purchase in the presentation of twentieth-century life. Advertising, baby advice, children's books, doctor's surgeries, educational arrangements, assume that we live in this way. It is hardly surprising to find that law also constitutes such a family form, which retains its power as an image against which relationships are judged. How does the constitutive element of law work? By projection of a stereotype of a relationship, such as marriage, a particular form is constituted. There are various elements to this. A specific model of marriage, that of a heterosexual union, submitted to legal ceremony, is the model for legislation. Family policies privilege this form, which is also upheld in judicial rhetoric. Relationships between lesbians, homosexual men, and non-sexual and cohabiting relationships are excluded. Furthermore, law constitutes the nature of the relationship within marriage (O'Donovan, 1979; 1985). Not only may this particular form of legally constituted relationship not respond to people's wishes, but the vision of alternative possibilities is limited.

Research refuting the notion of the idealised family has been widely published officially by government statisticians (CSO, *Social Trends*, 1991), and by feminist writers (Smart, 1984). But the potency of such myths should not be underestimated in a society where law makers are overwhelmingly male, middle-class, and belong to a generation whose mothers and wives are likely to live out the myth. Despite evidence that working-class women have always contributed to family finances, that lone mothers are less likely to work outside the home than married mothers (Martin and Roberts, 1984), that fathers living away from their children are unwilling to support them (1990: Cmnd 1263), the myth of the ideal family retains its grip on legislative imagination.

We are dealing with three different aspects: social changes within those family forms validated externally by law; explanations for law's retention of a specific family form that it constitutes; and the exclusion of relationships that do not conform to law's model. Drawing on Reich's (1964) work on the new property, Glendon (1977) contrasts the security derived from jobs and pensions with dependence on a family breadwinner. In Reich's view wealth is now largely based on earned income and jobs are also a source of status. For those without jobs their chief source of subsistence is welfare claims against government. Glendon contrasts this security with the insecurity of family life, in which reliance on a partner for income and status may be misplaced. According to this thesis, individuals look to employers or to the state for their economic security and status, and not to the family.

This 'new family' is contrasted with pre-modern, early modern, and nineteenth-century families. Whereas the former is characterised by fluidity, detachability and interchangeability of relationships, the last two are presented as having been stable with an emphasis on kinship ties rather than sexual love and personal happiness. Detailed research does not fully support this picture of past stability: short lifespan, hierarchy, economic dependence, lack of judicial divorce must also be brought into the picture. Change, however, within a particular family form – marriage – there has been.

Feminist writers have provided explanations for the constitution of a specific form of marriage in family law (Smart: 1984; Weitzman: 1981; 1985; Olsen: 1983; O'Donovan: 1985). It is not suggested that law is the immediate expression of male interests. But law assists in the reproduction of the dominant patriarchal social order, in particular by constituting a specific form of marriage, with different 'places' for wife and husband. It is this patriarchal arrangement, sustained by law, which ensures the social and economic insecurity of wives and mothers. It is for women to perform the unpaid work of child rearing which leaves them in a position of economic vulnerability. This work and the primacy of their domestic role, including a servicing of physical and emotional needs of others, ensures that women's interests are subordinated. They are the linchpin of what Olsen (1983: 1563) has called the 'altruistic, hierarchical, private family'.

Naffine (1990) adds a further dimension to this analysis by suggesting that the person behind law is the white middle-class male. Her examination is of the abstract individual who serves as an organising conceptual category in establishing law's impartiality. The argument is developed that the idea of an abstract individual is fundamentally misconceived, and that:

> law in fact anticipates and assumes a very particular type of social order in which a particular type of individual is thought to flourish. And it is this individual, not anyone whom law in fact endeavours to serve. (Naffine, 1990: 22)

The specific argument is that law, while purporting to deal with the abstract individual, projects a particular person – 'the man of law'. This is an individual who flourishes in, and is dominant in, the type of society conceived by law. Law reflects his priorities and concerns, and he finds law to be right. The gender of this person 'takes the form of an assertive, articulated, independent, calculating, competitive and competent man' (Naffine, 1990: 22). These are the qualities valued in a modern free-market society. Naffine does not claim that men constitute an undifferentiated category. She is at pains to distinguish those men who fail the test of middle-class masculinity, and who therefore derive fewer benefits than the man of law.

At the conclusion of her work Naffine finds a paradox at the heart of law. This resides in law's view of humanity. Although officially the legal subject is universal, in practice:

> [the] man of law is assumed to be a freestanding, autonomous creature, rationally self-interested and hardheaded; on the other hand he is a being who is assumed both to have and to need access to the values of Gemeinschaft, the family values, though he must not display them in his public, legal Gesellschaft life. (Naffine, 1991: 148)

This contradiction is presented as being at the centre of the liberal conception of society. It is to women that law assigns the job of holding the two halves together. The invisibility of women's work, the efforts of emotional succour, enable the legal man to appear in the public world of Gesellschaft free of encumbrances. This provides an explanation for law's continued constitution of a particular family form, however out of touch with the majority of lives. Naffine insists that the legal ideal of the person is not the creation of a few powerful men, rather it emanates from an impersonal, but patriarchal, social vision of what represents the good life, that of liberal political philosophy.

Feminist theory enables voices that are normally silenced by the more powerful legal voice to speak. Differing perspectives from those that dominate can be expressed. Dissent can be recognised. The final aspect, that of the exclusion of certain forms of relationship from law's constitution of the family, must now be considered.

The constitution of marriage and of parenthood in a specific context, that of a permanent, heterosexual relationship, is investigated in detail in Chapter 3. This has an effect on the constitution of sex and gender in which women and men are presented in a binary fashion as having opposed qualities and roles. It is not just that this has a limiting effect on ontological possibilities – the ways in which we see ourselves, how we project our futures – but those who cannot, or do not wish to, conform to relationships as legally constituted are stigmatised. This can be presented in liberal discourse as against liberty.

If It's Not a Family, What Is It?

Discussions of definitions and the nature of 'family' are many. The topic is central to the sociology of the family. As already stated, there is no one definition in law. Family law textbooks offer a variety of phrases: 'a group of persons related to each other by blood and/or marriage' (Hoggett and Pearl, 1987: 1). Various tests are suggested: a single household? Pooled resources? Should we look to demographers and anthropologists who offer various 'types': simple; nuclear; elementary; stem; biological; conjugal; extended; multiple-family household? These are analytical concepts, in which writers attempt to identify certain common and distinguishing features and then move on to generalisation. Such prototypes do not necessarily reflect individual experience. The legal problem is that despite idealisation of the nuclear, heterosexual family, there is no consistent model of what a family is. A court has declared that:

> in no case has the court found it possible to identify the necessary ingredient or quality that distinguishes a familial nexus from a nexus less than familial. The approach of the courts has been to look at the circumstances and then seek to answer the question: 'What would an ordinary person characterize the relationship as?' (*Sefton Holdings* v. *Cairns*, 1988: 109)

Examination of varying judicial pronouncements on the definition of family reveals no continuous thread. No consistent philosophy is to be found, rather a case-by-case reaction to differing legislative provisions. However, reference to popular morality or a common understanding does permeate the cases. This device of reference to common sense is used also by politicians. For example, Margaret Thatcher has said: 'Our grandparents and parents brought us up without trendy theories and didn't make a bad job of it' (*Daily Telegraph*, 13 October 1978). This type of pragmatism allows an avoidance of clarification. What follows is intended to illustrate this lack of open definition of the concept of family from legal materials. The Rent Act 1977 (sched. 1, para. 3) states that on the death of a tenant a statutory tenancy, in the absence of a surviving spouse, can devolve upon 'a person who was a member of the original tenant's family' residing with the tenant for six months prior to death. Where a man and a woman have lived together for some 20 years it has nevertheless been held as follows (on identical wording): 'To say of two people masquerading, as these two were, as husband and wife (there being no children to complicate the picture) that they were members of the same family, seems to be an abuse of the English language', and the court therefore denied the status of family membership to the survivor (*Gammans* v. *Ekins*, 1950). However, in a later case, 21 years of heterosexual cohabitation sufficed to enable the tenancy to pass to the surviving cohabitee. The word 'family' was 'not restricted to blood relationships and those created by the marriage ceremony', but must be considered in common parlance or the 'popular meaning or concept of the word' (*Dyson Holdings* v. *Fox*, 1975). But where there was no 'charade of marriage' because the couple did not conceal their status, the court refused to find that the ordinary or natural meaning of the expression 'member of a family' covered a man and a woman living together, as the test is 'what the ordinary man would say'. Although the couple had lived together for five years, the court felt the relationship lacked stability (*Helby* v. *Rafferty*, 1979). The test is whether the 'ordinary man' would recognise the relationship in question as establishing 'a broadly recognisable familial nexus' (*Carega Properties* v. *Sharratt*, 1979). But there is some doubt as to who precisely this man is: 'Do you listen to the vociferous minority or do you imagine what the silent majority might have said at a particular time?' (*Helby* v. *Rafferty*, 1979: 17).

As can be deduced, the courts have opted for reference to the 'ordinary man' as the arbiter of popular opinion, thus allowing changes in popular morality to be incorporated. This has been characterised as requiring the following question: 'What would the ordinary person characterise the relationship as?' (*Sefton Holdings* v. *Cairns*, 1988). But this reference to popular morality does not require a careful sampling of public opinion. Nor even is a jury polled for its opinion. Not only does it assume that the judiciary is in touch with public opinion, but it leaves open to the discretion of the judge the definition of popular morality, which may be confused with personal morality. There is an enormous number of different family worlds, as the empirical collation of statistics by official government agencies makes clear.

Scholars have pointed out that the existing approach of the courts is to give primacy to marriage or to parenthood. Thus Ghandi and MacNamee (1991: 114) comment on the revealing language used in a case where the status of family member was denied to the survivor of a relationship between two women who lived as sisters for 45 years. The court refused to find that a family relationship existed:

> Granted that 'family' is not limited to cases of a strict legal familial nexus, I cannot agree that it extends to a case such as this. It still requires, it seems to me, at least a broadly recognisable de facto familial nexus. This may be capable of being found and recognised as such by the ordinary man – where the link would be strictly familial had there been a marriage or where the link is through adoption of a minor, de jure or de facto, or where the link is 'step', or even where the link is 'in-law' or by marriage. But two strangers cannot, it seems to me, ever establish artificially for the purposes of this section a familial nexus by acting as brothers or as sisters, even if they call each other such and consider their relationship to be tantamount to that ... Nor in my view would they be recognised as familial links by the ordinary man. (*Sefton Holdings* v. *Cairns*, 1988, quoting *Ross* v. *Collins*, 1964)

Where legislation is more specific the reference to what the ordinary person thinks may be excluded by the detail of the language. The Housing Act 1985 (s. 113 (l) (2)) defines membership of a family as covering: spouse; living together as husband and wife; parent; grandparent; child; grandchild; brother; sister; uncle; aunt; nephew; niece. A member of the family can succeed to a council tenancy under the Act (s. 87), but a woman who shared a 'committed, monogamous, homosexual relationship' with another woman was denied succession to the tenancy (*Harrogate Borough Council* v. *Simpson,* 1986). Her argument was that the couple had lived together for a considerable period and that their relationship was such that it involved incidences of marriage such as long-term commitment, affection, sexual involvement, financial support. The judge's view was that 'the ordinary man and woman ... would in my opinion, not even remotely think of there being a true resemblance between these two very different states of affairs'. It is tempting to conclude as Ghandi and MacNamee have done that 'as in marriage an essential component of non-marital relationships which is needed to give rise to rights that might be termed familial is "natural heterosexual intercourse", which definitional excludes relationships between people of the same sex' (1991: 116).

Examination of the language used in *Gammans* v. *Ekins* (1950) reinforced the idea of a heterosexual, biological family, although not necessarily constituted by marriage. The couple had been known as married in their neighbourhood, and the woman had taken the man's name during the 20 years they had lived together. After her death he sought to prove that he was a member of her family. This was rejected by the court. But it was suggested that the presence of children in a cohabiting relationship might turn it into a family:

> it seems to me that as soon as children of two such parties, or one of them come into question, there may be said to be de facto an actual family consisting of children and the natural parent or parents of those children. It is then easy to see how the children could properly be brought within the expression 'family' according to the ordinary and popular meaning of the word. It is possible ... that in such a case either of the de facto parents could properly be held to be a member of the other's family ... (*Gammans* v. *Ekins,* 1950)

As an alternative to what 'the man in the street' thinks about the definition of the family, we might look to the functions of a relationship. The fulfilment of human needs, affection, shared domestic tasks, economic co-operation, are some of the work performed by the family. This approach has been taken by the New York Court of Appeals in the construction of rent control regulations. The words 'either the surviving spouse of the deceased tenant or some other member of the deceased tenant's family who has been living with the tenant' were read as including a homosexual partner. The couple had lived together for eleven years, and the court looked to the exclusivity and longevity of the relationship, the level of emotional and financial commitment, the way of life of the couple, how they had held themselves out to others as partners, and their mutual reliance. Since the policy of the regulations was the protection of family relationships, the denial of protection in this case would be to favour 'fictitious, legal distinctions or genetic history' over 'the reality of family life' (*Braschi* v. *Stahl Assocs*, 1989: 201).

Although functional criteria may be an advance on reference to that 'notoriously conservative individual' (Ghandi and MacNamee, 1991: 115) the reasonable, ordinary man in the street, nevertheless there are criticisms of this standard. The functional standard is still traditional marriage, albeit without heterosexuality. Discretion remains with the judiciary. There is an element of intrusion, with depictions of intimate life, not required of those who can claim a legal status. In other words, the specific model of traditional marriage is retained, but adapted to same-sex partners.

Bradney (1979) has suggested that the paucity of discussion among lawyers on the concept of family might be enriched by looking to sociological work. Three elements have been identified by Morgan (1977: 168). These are marriage, parenthood and residence. As can be discerned, the first two find their basis in status, legal and *de facto*. But the last is empirical.

Some 'family-like' quality can be found even by taking one element alone. The idea of residence as relevant has found its way into the law relating to children and step-parents. Statutory formulae place legal duties, particularly of financial support, on the stepparent who has treated the child as a 'child of the family' (Matrimonial Causes Act 1973, s. 52 (1). The phrase is also used in legislation on support after death: Inheritance (Provision for Family and Dependants) Act 1975; Fatal Accidents Act 1976 (as amended by the Administration of Justice Act 1982).

Examination of court decisions on the meaning of family in this context reveals reference to popular perceptions and common sense (Priest, 1984). The 'ordinary sensible citizen' has been called to aid, and the courts have advised avoiding 'the finer points of analysis in these cases' (*Re M*, 1980) probably because of definitional problems.

Prior to 1979 the Criminal Injuries Compensation Scheme, which exists to compensate victims of crime, excluded those victims who were living with the offender 'as members of the same family' at the time of the incident. This provision was used to deny compensation to those who suffered sexual or physical abuse as children, and also to other victims of family violence. It covered stepparents and *de facto* relationships and was not confined to the biological family.

Definitions of the family itself and of roles within it still encompass primarily the traditional, heterosexual nuclear family and its members. Benefits are often denied to non-traditional relationships. Three strategies on the part of courts faced with definitional problems have been identified: reference to popular morality; formal definition based on tradition; and a functional analysis to encompass those relationships that are said to share the essential characteristics of the traditional family. From this emerges a hierarchy of family forms, in which legal status attracts greatest recognition, particularly that of marriage. Parenthood, a concept legally defined, with a status element, is next in line for legal recognition, even where parents are not married. Heterosexual cohabiting relationships are recognised for some purposes, even where there are no children of the relationship, or of the 'family'. Relationships between lesbians and homosexual men are largely excluded, as are 'sister' or 'brother' arrangements between those seen by law as strangers.

Rules about roles and duties in the family, differentiating women, men, parents, children, family members and outsiders, underlie other social arrangements. Education, employment, welfare systems and commerce are affected. Substantial social benefits accrue to the privileged family form relating to housing, immigration, welfare, private insurance, child custody, access to children, rights of succession on death. The exclusion of those in non-traditional relationships is a major disbenefit. It may also be a denial of human rights. The International Covenant on Civil and Political Rights, of which the United Kingdom is a signatory, provides a standard against which legal treatment of the family can be measured. Article 23 provides:

1   The family is the natural and fundamental group unit of society and is entitled to protection by society and the state.
2   The right of men and women of marriageable age to marry and found a family shall be recognised.

Ghandi and MacNamee (1991) argue that the covenant, applicable to families in all regions of the world, takes account of cultural differences and accepts the non-essential nature of family structures. As we have already seen, English law takes an essentialist approach to the construction of the family. This involves the exclusion of certain people from family membership, on what the authors term 'arbitrary grounds' (1991: 105). The covenant requires that the exclusion of certain individuals or groups from family membership must be justified on 'objective and reasonable' grounds, and that the protection of family rights must be equal. The argument is that legal status is insufficient to ground the distinctions made in English law between different forms of relationship. The claim made by the authors is that marriage

is unjustifiably privileged in family law. Instead, an empirical, conse-
quential approach is proposed:

> Any distinctions made between people in family law should be
> based on an idea of the family that takes account of actual rela-
> tionships between individuals; on who is financially dependent on
> whom, on who lives with whom and for how long they have done
> so, on what has been shared in that relationship and what has not,
> on who had contributed what to the relationship and on who needs
> what after the relationship breaks down. (Ghandi and MacNamee,
> 1991: 127)

We may therefore conclude that the word 'family' has many
meanings and many contexts. We may also be aware that many people
have different and differing experiences of families. For some, these will
be validated by law. For others, their experiences are ignored or stigmatised. Although the question 'if it's not a family, what is it?' is
apposite, a technical legal answer based on formal law, and legal
status, may always exclude stigmatised relationships. Thus law privileges
certain forms and denies recognition and benefits to others, while simultaneously denying that a coherent definition of a family exists. This
permits the continuation of a subtext of patriarchal conformity. It does
not necessarily support the family as the 'building block of society'.

Familial Ideology

What is the ideology of the family which contributes to the maintenance of present structures? For evidence of views of law-makers we
can turn to the statements of politicians and of the judiciary – the traditional establishment. The family is presented in the Britain of the
1990s as the bedrock of traditional values and common sense. Thus the
individualism contained in economic programmes is to be countered
by the reassuring image of the nation as an extended family. At the same
time, a search for shared values is apparent: 'Let us do all in our power
to see one another's point of view and to widen the common ground
on which we stand' (Thatcher, *Daily Telegraph*, 13 October 1978).

In political rhetoric the family serves many purposes. It is totem,
emblem of stability, reassurance and common sense. It can be used to
reject challenges to established authority and to castigate critics as
'trendy'. It also serves to be made guilty, to be blamed for crime rates,
delinquency, illiteracy. Yet it can stand against the state as bulwark
against intrusion and interference. Thus Ferdinand Mount, one-time
Cabinet office advisor:

The family's most dangerous enemies may not turn out to be those who have openly declared war. It is so easy to fight against the blatant cruelty of collectivist dictators ... It is less easy to fight against the armies of those who are 'only here to help' – those who claim to come with the best intention but come armed, all the same, with statutory powers and administrative instruments: education officers, children's officers ... welfare workers and all the other councils ... which claim to know best how to manage our private concerns. (Mount, 1982: 173)

The family does not have to establish its credentials, its origins, its sources – it just is whatever it is. It contains, as Goodrich (1990: 41) says of law, the tradition of inescapable institutions – repetition. It reproduces itself and leaves its traces on our lives, in our relations with others, in our ethical views. In its rituals, its special forms of address, its 'heritable form of repetition' it constitutes everyday life. The idea of the familiar is rooted in family. In certain senses family is outside the law, separate from it. As one former government minister puts it, the family:

poses strength and resilience, not least in adversity. Loyalty to the family ranks highest of all, higher even than loyalty to the state. It is no accident ... that dictatorships, whether of the Left or the Right, seek first to devalue and then to destroy the family. (*Daily Telegraph*, 15 May 1991)

That the family might abuse its younger or physically weaker members is not contemplated in this discourse. Chapter 5 discusses the vulnerability of children to the power of adults.

It is for women to keep the family together despite abuse, as Margaret Thatcher has made clear. She represents this not only as a moral duty but also as self-interest. So long as the nuclear family remains 'the reservoir of moral, philosophical and social values' (Thomas, 1991), women will have a secure position.

Children have been encouraged to grow up faster and to see themselves as independent of parents. Parents have been told by self-appointed experts that their duties to each other and to their children should be balanced by more emphasis on self-fulfilment. In other words, we have been the birth of the permissive society. Has this benefitted women? Women know that society is founded on dignity, reticence and discipline. We know instinctively that the dis-integration of society begins with the death of idealism and convention. We know that for our society as a whole, and especially to the children, much depends upon the family unit remaining secure and respected (quoted in Thomas, 1991: 26 July 1982)

The mythology of the holy family as place of love and security, outside and free from law is represented in legal texts: 'for that my house is the subject place for my refuge, my safety and comfort of my family' *The Case of the Prerogative of the King in Saltpetre* (*Cokes Report*, vol 12: 13, quoted by Goodrich and Hachamotivitch, 1991: 165). That it may also be a place where husband procures a stranger to rape his wife 'to punish her for past misconduct', using another's body to 'provide the physical means to that end' (*R* v. *Cogan and Leak*, 1976: 221) cannot be represented in this fictive eloquence.

The place of refuge, as identified by Goodrich and Hachamotivitch (1991: 166) has its imagery in the tending of one's garden. 'That is the Englishman's fate, but at least the law protects that secluded privacy, that walled garden, that patch of obsessively native soil so beloved of the English.' The law of trespass is dedicated to this defence of property, of the soil:

> No man can set his foot upon my ground without my licence, but he is liable to an action, though the damage be nothing: which is proved by every declaration in trespass, where the defendant is called upon to answer for bruising the grass and even treading upon the soil. (*Entick* v. *Carrington*, 1765: 1066)

The sanctity of garden, castle, home, cottage is reiterated again and again. It is free from invasion by strangers, or even law, for under common law 'the house of everyone is his castle' (*Semayne's Case*, 1604). As regards the conduct of 'domestic life, the rule is that Courts of Law should not intervene except upon occasion. It is far better that people should be left free' (*Re Agar-Ellis*, 1883: 335). Home and refuge being, in the eyes of law, identical, it is for the inhabitants to sort out their disagreements. 'The parties themselves are advocates, judges, courts, sheriff's officers and reporter. In respect of these promises each house is a domain into which the King's writ does not seek to run, and to which its officers do not seek to be admitted'(*Balfour* v. *Balfour*, 1919). The promises involved were of financial support.

Unfortunately, for those who suffer abuse in the home it is not a place of refuge. They are caught in familial ideology prescribing love, trust and dependence in which they share, even as small children. And because the refuge, castle or garden is to be secluded from law, help may be slow to arrive. This problem of ideology and intervention remains central in family law.

Readers may note that familial ideology is not dependent on marriage. Cohabiting partners, particularly where there are children, are also seen as constitutive of a family – its values and ideologies. For example, in cases of physical or sexual abuse whether or not the family is constituted by marriage is an irrelevant question. The issue is concerned with legal intervention in 'the sanctity of the home'. It seems that we answer the question 'if it is not a family, what is it?' by acknowledging familiar features. But without legal recognition certain family forms are denied privileges that law confers on approved relationships.

4
Marriage – Sacred Union or Determinable Contract?

Modern critics of the legally structured family have 'unbuilt' the structure and subjected each part to scrutiny. This deconstruction is presented as an opening of a black box, of which the contents, their shapes and sizes, how they fitted in and together, were unknown. The black box has been found to contain some nasty pieces. The figures do not necessarily fit together, or fit at all. This unbuilding has refuted many grand theories of the family, particularly those of the structural/functionalists who built their theoretical edifice on the notion of fit between the nuclear family on the one hand and economy and state on the other (Parsons, 1949, 1968). Deconstructionists who subjected family members to scrutiny have also examined the legal structure. Legal marriage, in particular, has suffered a severe critique (Weitzman, 1981; Smart, 1984; O'Donovan, 1985). As a contract, so presented in legal discourse throughout the history of common law, it cannot stand. Its terms are not negotiated by the parties, but prescribed by law. It is not a contract freely entered into by any adult but is open only to certain persons under specified conditions according to law. Termination of marriage can occur only as denoted by law, and not by the partners. Within the legal married state, law's prescriptions allocate roles ascriptively, according to gender, and not according to the wishes of the partners. Legal marriage requires the sacrifice of personal autonomy but not on equal terms for the parties. An ascriptive quality, gender, is incorporated in the legal institution, as we saw in the discussion of the marital rape exemption. This differentiation of the partners produces inequality.

This critique is well known. It has affected some partners, to whom legal marriage is available, who have opted to avoid the institution. Of the 27 per cent of children born outside legal marriage in 1990, 73 per cent were registered in the names of both parents. Not all of these couples are marriage rejecters; perhaps not many are. According to *Social Trends* 53 per cent of couples marrying in 1987 had previously cohabited (1991: 2.17). However the critique of marriage has been taken sufficiently seriously by some writers who advise their readers not to attend weddings (Barrett and McIntosh,1982: 143). This chapter is interested in the question why, notwithstanding the critique of legal marriage, people continue to marry and to uphold the institution. I argue that this is so because marriage has a sacred, magical status. Many of those who do not marry nevertheless enter into quasi-marriage, and look to law to resolve subsequent disputes over children or property. Homosexual partners regret their inability to marry and confirm the institution in their quest to do so. We are dealing with something deeply embedded and, although its legal form may be criticised, its continued survival must be acknowledged. Marriage as a sacred institution is discussed in detail later.

Where the notion of marriage as free contract is rejected, writers tend to use the word 'institution' instead, as has been done above, and this may be an appropriate word. When one enters an institution one does so on terms set by that body, one is bound by the rules to which one consents on entry. However, the membership may collectively agree a change of rules. It is not easy to apply this analysis to marriage. It is law, not the partners, which lays down the rules, not only of entry, but also of membership. Collective agreement on the alteration of the rules by the partners is not possible. We are up against something not easily analysed in institutional terms. Marriage has contractual and institutional elements, but it is also *sui generis*, a law unto itself.

Getting Married – Who Can and Who Cannot?

Sections 11 and 12 of the Matrimonial Causes Act 1973 prescribe indirectly the conditions for getting married. By declaring certain marriages null and void, the Act indicates what the conditions of validity are. Briefly, those to be married must be female and male respectively, making marriage the paradigm of the sexual contract. They must be over 16, not already married to another at the time of the ceremony, not previously related by blood or marriage within specified limits, and not legally capable of entering into polygamy. They must consent freely. Breach of any of these conditions means that the marriage is void, that is, from the beginning it has never existed legally. However, such a void marriage may still attract the powers of matrimonial courts to make orders for children and finances.

Certain other legally defective marriages, namely those defined as voidable, tell us more. The ceremony of marriage is one constitutive act. It must conform to certain procedural and spatial requirements. It must be entered into freely. The second constitutive act is sexual consummation, after the ceremony. Without both these acts, the marriage is either void or voidable. Its sexual nature is now clear. Incapacity or wilful refusal to consummate, and the following four grounds relating to consent, render a marriage voidable, provided certain time requirements are fulfilled: lack of valid consent because of incapacity to understand the nature of the marriage contract, or because of duress, or mistake, or otherwise; mental disorder within the meaning of the Mental Health Act 1983 of such a kind or to such an extent as to create unfitness for marriage; communicable venereal disease, or pregnancy by a third person, neither having been revealed to the other spouse before the ceremony. For ethical reasons the court may refuse a nullity decree if the petitioner, knowing that the marriage could be annulled, so behaved towards the respondent as to lead him/her to believe that no petition would be made, and where it would be unjust to grant the decree.

These indirectly derived requirements of marriage tell us about the form of relationship constituted by law under the label marriage. This is a sexually differentiated union of a pair, old enough, and able, to decide to change their legal status, who promise monogamy (or serial polygamy), and who are free of other marital partners. They must engage in one act of heterosexual intercourse after the ceremony to consummate the marriage.

Certain formalities are specified for a marriage ceremony, the absence of which may make the marriage void. It is not for the couple to decide to marry under water or on a mountain, for to 'knowingly and wilfully intermarry' in breach of formalities makes the marriage void (s. 11 (a) (iii)). These specified formalities include certification, solemnisation by an authorised person, or in a holy place. Recommended formalities are the consent of parents where one party is under eighteen, and observation of the Marriage Act 1949, but failure to respect these does not lead to annulment, although in the latter case there may be a criminal sanction.

Getting married, from the legal standpoint, is an uneasy mixture of two acts freely performed by the united pair, and legal regulation. The performative acts by the couple are their voluntary taking of one another as husband or wife, with all that these terms connote; the sexual act, after the ceremony is the seal of the union. Law regulates entry into marriage, the ceremony and the validity of both. In that sense law constitutes the marriage. As will be shown later, this constitution extends to other aspects of marriage and affects termination.

Law Constitutes Marriage

The effect of the provisions outlined above is to limit the formation of marriage and also its forms. Heterosexual relations are privileged by their capacity to attract legal consequences. Not only must the partners be female and male respectively, but they must enter a sexual relationship of a particular kind. Heterosexual and transsexual relationships cannot be marriages, nor can group unions. Marriages recognised in other cultures, such as polygamous marriages or child marriages, are void. After the marriage at least one sexual act of penetration of the vagina by the penis must occur for the marriage to be consummated.

The language of the law is interesting. To consume a body with mouth and teeth is cannibalism. Consummation with a sexual organ gives a different form of pleasure. 'Only the marriage contract can turn use of sexual property in which "one is really made a res fungibilis to the other", into the use of a person. But it is the husband who has use of a person, not the wife' (Pateman, 1988a: 172). The male marital right can be confirmed in the past exemption of husbands from the criminal law of rape in relation to their wives. The marriage contract establishes the possession of the wife's body by her husband, but she has no corresponding right. After consummation further heterosexual acts are assumed to take place in accordance with male desire. It is evident that the law approves heterosexuality in marriage but withholds its constitutive power from other relationships not legally approved.

The requirement of consummation places primacy on penetrative sex, an act constitutive of masculinity. As Moran (1990: 171) points out, consummation 'is of considerable significance as a site relating to the emergence of male heterosexual sexuality within the institution of marriage'. Reported cases reveal bizarre knowledge against which questions were asked about 'how long, and how wide, and how far, and whether, and what'. Determination of the standard, the norm, against which to measure the answers created a 'knowledge' of male sexuality and a discourse of normal masculinity. Law's insistence on consummation as the final performative act constituting marriage marginalises other sexual practices. The missionary position, in which the woman lies under the man and facing him in readiness for coition, has been privileged in this discourse. The position is so-called because it was introduced by missionaries, along with clothing, to primitive peoples, where it was virtually unknown, in the course of colonisation. In 1969 there still remained six state jurisdictions in the United States where a woman could be awarded a divorce if her husband required her to take part in an act of sexual intercourse with him in any other than the missionary position (Golanty and Harris, 1982: 165). Although marriage law does not demand that the missionary position is adopted for consummation, it is clear that non-penetrative sexual activity is insufficient.

The language of consummation has sacramental associations, not only with marriage but also with eucharist. To account fully for the resistance of marriage to deconstruction and critique we must consider its religious and sacramental character. English family law draws its model of marriage from Judaeo-Christian traditions. This model is of marriage for life, to one person of the other sex, a heterosexual relationship. Although divorce is permitted leading to 'serial monogamy', polygamy is not. Endogamy, and marriage outside the immediate kin group, is enforced through prohibition on marriage within certain degrees of relationship. But above all marriage takes its character as an institution in which the sexes are united and opposed. Its representation as a sacrament makes this appear natural.

The sacred character of marriage as an institution calls on a past, understood and shared tradition, and on an eternal future, a perpetuity. Marriage is an emblem of continuity, of reproduction of the race, of the recruitment of new members, of the creation of new units, of generation from one generation to another. Not only are sexual needs to be met but marriage is the place for the veneration of motherhood, for deference to patriarchy, for the continuance of tradition, learned yet known anew by each generation and in each generative act.

Through marriage the couple become one flesh, one body. In legal terms, this biblical notion takes form in the constitution of the couple as a unit headed by the husband. This was one reason why the husband could not be guilty of rape of the wife – he could not rape himself – his 'other half'. The wife was 'Adam's rib' made by God from the first man, and therefore a small part of the male. As a sacrament, an indissoluble union of mystical and metaphysical nature, marriage is eternal. Despite the introduction of divorce by the 'moderns' in 1857, marriage is forever, in the sense that it is still sought by the great majority of citizens. Its indissoluble and immutable qualities remain in memories, experiences, generative acts, even of those who have terminated one union and moved on to another. Marriage is, on this understanding, not only sacrament but also sacrifice. With consummation God enters into the act of heterosexual intercourse, and the sacrifice is made. Although this may no longer be a sacrifice of female virginity to male sexual desire, there is a sacrifice of autonomy, albeit on unequal terms. The 'consummation most devoutly to be wished for' is the final performative act of consecration of the marriage. The primal act of heterosexual intercourse is to be repeated as a generative act ad infinitum.

The nature of the marital sexual relationship can be deduced from reported cases disputing consummation. The definitive form of sexual relations is 'male penetration of the female body: intercourse must be ordinary and complete, not partial and imperfect' for consummation (*D-E* v. *A-G*, 1845); there must be full penetration, which may be verified; medical inspection can be asked for (*Cowen* v. *Cowen*, 1945); according to Chitty (1834) for male capacity there must be erectio, intromissio and ejaculatio in vaginam; penetration for a short time without any ejaculation does not amount to consummation (*W (orse K)* v. *W*, 1967). The courts have developed a precise calibration of heterosexual male performance, a 'penile economy' (Moran, 1990). The phallus is constructed as the organising principle of the sex act (Campbell, 1980: 5). The woman's participation is required only as object, provided she has an adequate vagina for penetration. Heterosexual intercourse is normal, the only approved form of sexual behaviour. The norm specifies how we should behave. The pleasures of the phallus are the pleasures of sex. Penetration defines sexual intercourse in law, family and criminal. The female orgasm is constructed as mysterious, possibly inexistent, maternity is female pleasure. Sexual pleasure received from physical closeness, from bodily contact, but not from penetration, does not exist or denotes female frigidity. Yet the birth of children is not essential to the validity of marriage; contraception, including the penile sheath, is not inimical to consummation (*Baxter* v. *Baxter*, 1948).

It is not only in the constitution of phallic sexuality as essential to the consummation of marriage that the judiciary are required to pronounce on norms and the normal. Divorce may also raise this. Where the question of what is reasonable to expect in terms of frequency of sexual intercourse was raised, Lord Justice Ormrod said, 'it seems to me quite impossible for any court to find that the refusal by a wife to have sexual intercourse more often than once a week is unreasonable' (*Mason* v. *Mason*, 1980). This resulted in popular interest in the sexual habits of the judiciary, and telephone calls by newspapers to their wives to inquire their opinions.

The story of marriage as an institution in which the sexes are united and opposed relates to the uncovering of the sexual contract. Not only is a particular form of marriage constituted, with a delineation of social roles and hierarchy, but marriage has much to say about the meaning of masculinity and femininity. Marriage establishes 'orderly access by men to women's bodies' according to Pateman (1988a: 2). This law of male sex-right embodies women as sexual beings. Although personal autonomy over sexuality has largely been won by women today, elements of the history of marriage remain. The story helps to understand what it means to be masculine or feminine in modern civil society. No matter how much we try to avoid replicating patriarchal marital relations, these are reproduced in the institution of marriage. As Pateman points out, 'the social and legal meaning of what it is to be a "wife" stretches across class and racial differences' (1988a: 18). Despite this critique of marriage, there are those excluded by the legal institution who wish to enter it. Their exclusion is necessary to maintain the present constitution, for the entry into marriage of partnerships between homosexual men or lesbians, of triads or polygamists, would not only alter the sacred character of the institution but the very definition, the constitution, the understanding from time immemorial. For this reason the desire for participation by the excluded must not necessarily be regarded as confirmation of traditional marriage. There are a number of reasons for wanting to marry. Some of these may be concerned with the social functions that legal recognition of a relationship serves. We need to ask which aspects of the married state are being sought by those excluded: security, permanence, legal guarantees, external recognition, performative acts, mutual obligation, gender roles, family foundation, social approval of sexuality, obligation of trust and love, non-interference from outside, privacy, children? We may then be able to set about disentangling the reasons why law treats marriage as a sacred, non-negotiable state, rather than as a private agreement. Law might then reconstitute its role and limit itself to certain functions of adjustment and protection, where necessary.

Excluded Viewpoints

Examination of those categories of persons excluded from marriage throws light on the cultural meaning of the institution. It is not being suggested that marriage is so benign an institution that it ought to be available to all. Opinions on this differ. Carol Smart (1984) favours the abolition of marriage on the grounds that, as presently constituted, it is oppressive to women. In her view it should be replaced by individual contracts. Carole Pateman (1988a) sees marriage as contaminated by patriarchal meaning and mastery; she is opposed, however, to its replacement by contract, which she sees as reductive of persons to interchangeable individuals in the market. That individual within market society is also patriarchally constructed. Escaping from marriage may not be easy. Even those who deliberately eschew the institution find themselves looking to it as a model for certain aspects of their personal lives, to the example familiar to most from childhood, reading or representation. It is hard to escape the iconography of saintly motherhood, authoritative father, the holy family. These venerated icons inform our ways of seeing, our thinking, even for those rejecting them. As the place of idealised intimacy, security, sexuality and stability, marriage remains the primordial model of personal relations. Hence those excluded wish to claim right of entry to this sacred terrain.

Transsexual Marriage
Transsexuals may wish to marry in their new gender identity, but in English law they cannot do so. A marriage between persons who are not respectively male and female is void under the Matrimonial Causes Act 1973 s. 11 (c). Being male or female is not an open question in law, nor will law accept a social answer based on desires, appearance, psychology or surgery. Sex is legally taken to be determined at birth and 'marriage is a relationship which depends on sex rather than gender'. Only those capable of engaging in 'natural heterosexual intercourse' can marry (*Corbett* v. *Corbett*, 1971). That this discourse privileges a certain form of relationship and of sexuality is clear. Where gender identity and personal characteristics are at odds with chromosomes, genitals and gonads, the legal definition of sex insists on a biological test, even where the latter two attributes have been surgically altered. In other words, sex is not a matter of choice, but in law is an essential characteristic biologically determined. Some absurdities result, as not

everyone can be classified on an either/or basis. There are persons with
a mixture of, or both, sex organs and attributes (O'Donovan, 1985, Ch.
3). The assumption of a sexual binary system into which all individuals can be fitted at birth underlies not only family law but also
criminal law, employment law and sex discrimination law, where the
family law approach has been adopted. The legal belief is that science
supports this binary approach. Yet the scientific and social scientific
work in the area leads to the conclusion that sexual attributes are best
described as a continuum rather than as absolutes. Hormones, in
particular, support this conclusion, which is also based on the variety
of factors that go to make up the concept of an individual's sex.

Criticism of the biological essentialism which underpins the legal view
of sex has been directed largely at two aspects: the reasoning adopted;
and the consequences in humanistic terms. In reasoning in an essentialist fashion, and in positing biological sex as the basis of marriage,
the court in *Corbett* (1971) took a binary attack. However, it is possible
to use a cluster-concept approach to ascertain a person's sex, by looking
to a variety of characteristics, including social and psychological
factors, and then to decide according to the preponderance. Furthermore, queries have been raised about the foundation of marriage on
sex rather than on gender, as other western states have based marriage
on the latter. For example, in Sweden post-operative transsexuals can
marry in their new gender (Bradley, 1990: 154).

More fundamental criticisms have been directed at the denial of the
humanity of transsexuals who wish to marry or to be legally recognised
in their new identity. Challenges to English law have been made
under the European Convention on Human Rights before the European
Court of Human Rights. Although that court has upheld the criteria
adopted in English law as 'the traditional concept of marriage', nevertheless the foundation of marriage on the biological sex of the
parties was strongly criticised by the four dissenting judges in *Cossey*
v. *UK* (1991). In an earlier case, *Rees* v. *UK* (1987) the court refused to
find any violation of the rights of a transsexual who had been refused
a new birth certificate and who wished to be able to marry.

Although English law remains in place, the dissenting judgments in
Cossey, and alterations in laws of other state parties to the European
Convention enabling full recognition of the new identity of transsexuals, suggest that change may eventually occur. Judge Martens
based his dissenting opinion on humanistic principles of dignity,
freedom and privacy. In his analysis marriage is 'far more than a
union that legitimates sexual intercourse and aims at procreating'. Not
only is it a legal institution but also 'a societal bond', and a 'species of
togetherness in which intellectual, spiritual and emotional bonds are
at least as essential as the physical ones'. This last phrase points up the
paradox that marriage is reduced by traditionalist analysis to no more

than a physical relationship for which one is qualified only by ascriptive biological criteria; yet persons who undergo surgery to qualify in conformity with biology are nevertheless unqualified as 'not really' a woman or a man. As the other three dissenters in *Cossey* pointed out, the post-operative transsexual cannot marry either as woman or as man because, after surgery, neither the former sex nor the new sex enables qualification. On humane grounds the right to marry, contained in article 12 of the European Convention, should be respected. The solution is to respect the individual's choice of sex and to permit marriage in the new category. This writer, however, queries the notion of sexual category and whether it is necessary to a legal concept of stable relationship, at present called marriage.

According to Judge Martens, 14 state parties to the European Convention make provision for legal recognition of the new sexual identity of a post-operative transsexual. These include Belgium, Denmark, Finland, France, Germany, Italy, Luxemburg, Portugal, Spain, Sweden, The Netherlands and Turkey. This suggests that the notion of eternal biology as the foundation of family may be changing. Transsexuals are boundary crossers. Their behaviour illuminates what it means to 'pass' as a man or a woman, and the degree to which we do this on a daily basis whatever our biology. The significance and the rootedness of our notions of femininity or masculinity become apparent. Perhaps this is why transsexuals are perceived as threatening traditional marriage and unsettling the eternal biological family.

Homosexual Marriage

Homosexual marriage is void, since the parties do not qualify under the Matrimonial Causes Act 1973, s. 11 (c) as male and female respectively. Unlike transsexuals, homosexuals do not claim heterosexual union as privileged by traditional marriage laws. It is unlikely therefore that the question of the validity of homosexual marriage will be put to a court, as the appearance of the parties at the ceremony may preclude its occurrence. If a marriage ceremony does take place it will probably be legally regarded as a sham and therefore the courts will refuse to notice it for purposes of invalidating it or dealing with issues of finances or property.

Denmark has enacted legislation which permits relationships between homosexuals to be legalised and socially recognised. In 1989 a special legal regime, the 'registered partnership' was introduced, in which couples of the same sex may register their relationship. Act no 372 states that registration of partnership carries the same legal consequences as marriage, with certain exceptions detailed in the legislation. The Act provides that where Danish law refers to 'marriage' or 'spouse', these references will include registered partnerships and partners thereto. Thus it follows that many of the privileges attached to heterosexual marriage are now extended to registered, same-sex, partnerships. However, where sex-specific words are used in legislation, such as 'husband' or 'wife', or where spouses are defined by sex, subsequent provisions do not apply to the partnership (Nielsen, 1990: 299). In other words, Danish law still foresees circumstances in which traditional, biologically differentiated relationships retain legal significance.

According to Nielsen (1990: 298) the general purpose of the legislation is to manifest social acceptance of a relationship between partners of the same sex, to create a legal institution recognising this and conferring the same rights and duties as those pertaining to marriage. There are other social goals: permitting expression of wishes and choice; improving the stability of homosexual relationships; allowing a choice between registration or informal relationship; recognition of permanent relationships for state-regulated matters such as housing, immigration, pensions and entitlement to work. Marriage, which is perceived by Danish social policy as the 'best juridical frame for the family', is the model for same-sex registered partnerships. Danish Marriage Acts, laws on succession, tax, pension and social security cover registered partners. Dissolution is as for divorce.

The major area of distinction in Danish law between registered partnership and legal marriage concerns children. Registered partners may not have joint custody of a child, nor may they jointly adopt a child. The biological child of one partner cannot be adopted by the other, as in stepparent adoption. 'The legislator considered it best for a child to have a 'father' and a 'mother' (Nielsen, 1990: 305). Danish law acknowledges a form of relationship usually denied recognition in western legal systems. It is presented rhetorically as an improvement in human rights. Such legality is not extended to heterosexual or homosexual informal cohabitation, because marriage or registration are seen as options which have been rejected, but which remain available. In other words the partners can choose to attach legal consequences to their relationships. It is noteworthy that marriage remains the legal institution that is a model for alternatives.

Polygamous Marriage

Dyadic, monogamous, heterosexual relationships are privileged by the law of marriage. Triad or group marriage is not possible, nor is polyandry or polygamy. Not only are bigamous marriages void under the Matrimonial Causes Act 1973, s. 11 (c), but they may give rise to criminal prosecution. Bigamy is a tribute to traditional marriage in that it mimics the marriage ceremony. Like other marriages classified void, the bigamous marriage attracts court jurisdiction over children and finances under the Matrimonial Causes Act 1973, s. 21 (1). The purpose of criminal prosecution for deliberately and knowingly becoming a bigamist is unclear. It may be that the law was designed to protect the female partner deceived by a male bigamist and whose consent to sexual intercourse was based on the supposed marriage. But the law is more general and covers all bigamists, deceivers or not. A more likely explanation is that a public official is deceived and a public record falsified.

It is not the purpose here to argue for an extension of legal marriage to plural relationships, but to highlight the present conception of marriage. Monogamy has been justified in the Judaeo-Christian tradition by reference to holy texts and to origins. In the recent past, where monogamy was imposed by law in British colonies in Hong Kong and Singapore, this was done in the name of women's rights. The Muslim religious tradition claims polygamy as a male right, and even a duty.

Where a person normally domiciled in a state that permits polygamous marriage marries in accordance with the law of such a state then recognition of the marriage in English law is possible (Pearl, 1986). Where such a man lives with several wives in England or Wales, limited legal acknowledgement of the status of the parties follows. For example, although there are no problems concerning the status of children or state allowances for them, a plurality of wives may not be claimed as individual beneficiaries of state contributory benefits. However if the claim relates to basic social security for those in need, second and subsequent wives are treated as additions to the household (Pearl, 1986: 49–50). Potentially polygamous marriage contracted abroad where there is only one actual wife is permitted to a man with an English domicile (*Hussain* v. *Hussain*, 1982). The Law Commission (1985, Cmnd 9595) has recommended the removal of the sex discrimination implicit in this rule. We are faced with increasing cultural pluralism which raises questions about the traditional legal response.

Cultural and Historical Particularities

In *Cossey* Judge Martens expressed the view that the European Court of Human Rights has a 'mission to protect the individual against the collectivity and to do so by elaborating common standards'. While we may applaud this endeavour, the problem of establishing pluralist standards remains with us. The judge also said that 'the Court should take great care not to yield too readily to arguments based on a country's cultural and historical particularities'.

The advent of immigrants with their own cultural definitions of marriage into English society puts pressure on traditional notions, as do social changes relating to transsexuality and homosexuality. Yet tradition is not immutable. Until the Age of Marriage Act 1929 English law held to the canon law ages of marriage of 12 for girls, and 14 for boys. Since then the age of marriage has been 16 for both partners, which corresponds to the age of consent to sexual intercourse for women and to that of medical consent (Sexual Offences Act 1956, s. 56 (1); Family Law Reform Act 1969, s. 8 (1)). Family law maintains its concept of the marriage age by holding void a marriage contracted abroad by a person with an English domicile where either party is underage (*Pugh* v. *Pugh*, 1951) and by immigration rules which preclude the entry into the United Kingdom of underage persons as spouses (Pearl, 1986: 87–8). However the marriage abroad of two Nigerian domiciliaries has been recognised despite the wife's age of 13, (*Mohamed* v. *Knott*, 1969). The judges have discretion to refuse recognition in 'particularly repugnant cases which are offensive to the conscience of the court, in line with the formula laid down by Simon P in *Cheni* v. *Cheni* (1962) (Poulter, 1986: 2.17).

What is implicit in these rules is cultural recognition of certain forms of relationship which are dignified as legal marriage, and which restrict acknowledgement of other relationships. Immigrants coming from another culture bring their own definitions of personal relations, of appropriate conduct, of expectations and values. For the first generation – those arriving from elsewhere – English law is willing to encompass their beliefs, largely by use of the legal construct, domicile. But the second generation, domiciled in England or Wales, are expected to conform to English law. This group finds itself caught between cultures. English family law based on religious tradition may not accord with their upbringing, but the immigrant tradition may be based on patriarchy, obedience to the authority of the family, arranged marriage, which does not accord with developing individualism.

Cases on arranged marriage illustrate the pressures on the children of immigrants, usually those from the Indian subcontinent. Such marriages, rooted in culture and religion, are compacts between families, whose own status and honour are involved. Arranged marriages normally take place with the tacit consent of the partners but issues of consent have been raised in English courts. If either party to a marriage does not validly consent to it because of duress, the marriage is voidable (Matrimonial Causes Act 1973 s. 12). English courts have shown uneasiness faced with petitions for nullity based on duress. In *Singh* v. *Singh* (1971) a Sikh girl of 17 went through a ceremony of marriage in a register office with a Sikh man of 21. Her parents arranged the marriage and she met the man shortly before the ceremony. She refused to go through a religious ceremony or to consummate the marriage and petitioned for nullity on grounds of parental duress. The Court of Appeal rejected the petition on the grounds that there was no evidence of actual fear on her part, or of immediate danger to life, liberty and limb. The reasoning of the court seems to have been that duress cannot exist where a petitioner attends a marriage ceremony and says the appropriate words. Such fear is either irrational and therefore unworthy of judicial notice, or non-existent as held in *Singh*.

This narrow approach, denying the existence of duress where a ceremony takes place and thus rendering nugatory the provision of the law, was followed in *Singh* v. *Kaur* (1981). The husband was told by his parents that refusal to comply with their wishes would necessitate giving up his job in the family business. He had no knowledge of the girl to whom he was married but the Court of Appeal held he was aware of the choices involved and it could not be said that fear vitiated his consent: 'he has to make up his mind, as an adult, whether to go through the marriage or whether to withstand the pressure put upon him by his family'.

It now appears that the Court of Appeal has broadened its approach by adopting the simple test of whether or not the petitioner's will has been so coerced as to vitiate consent. In *Hirani* v. *Hirani* (1982) the parents of an Indian Hindu woman objected to her friendship with a Muslim man. They threatened to expel her from home unless she married a Hindu man unknown to them and to their daughter. In the end she married the man in both civil and religious ceremonies, while making clear her unhappiness. Although she lived with the husband for six weeks the marriage was not consummated. The court held that her will was overborne and her consent vitiated. Whether the decision was motivated out of sympathy for 'a young girl, wholly dependent on her parents' who was not classified as 'an adult', or whether it signals a more general sympathy for children caught in a culture clash is not clear. It is likely that the courts will continue to approach issues of pluralism, of a variety of marriage traditions, in a pragmatic, commonsensical fashion.

Ideals about marriage in English law draw on the sacramental, the antique, the eternal, the timeless, unwritten understandings, biblical tradition. In a discussion of the law of nullity the Law Commission refers to what is 'unwelcome to the Church' (1970, no. 33, para. 24 (b)). But the other reference group in this document is 'many people', 'people not necessarily belonging to the Church'. They are the custodians of tradition, of what is immutable and yet can change. Law makers may look to 'what is normally regarded', for responses to 'social and moral problems, the answer to which must depend on public opinion'. Values and answers lie with these custodians as there 'are some matters of conviction on which men hold strong feelings of right and wrong though they cannot place their fingers on any particular reason for this conviction'.

Ideology of Marriage

Challenges to traditional marriage from the excluded raise the question of why this particular union, this particular form of relationship, comes under the gaze of the law to be privileged as legal marriage. An answer has already been given by reference to the timeless, the eternal, the antique, unwritten understanding. Marriage is not an essential unit for parenthood or for child care, as lone parents and cohabiting couples bear witness. Other legal systems have attempted answers by broadening the definition of marriage to encompass transsexuals, by creating new forms of relationship recognised by law – such as Danish homosexual registered partnership, by giving a legal status to hetero-sexual cohabiting couples through legislation (the New South Wales De Facto Relationships Act 1984). In such answers marriage remains the model to which other relationships aspire.

Rationalistic analysis of the legal privileging of marriage over other relationships points to the statistics on cohabitation and to the numbers of children born outside marriage (27 per cent in 1990). Consider, however, the numbers marrying: the United Kingdom had the highest rate in the European Community in 1988, at 6.9 marriages per 1,000 eligible population, equalled only by Portugal (1991, *Social Trends*, 21: 2.11). Legal marriage thrives as an institution, and those excluded pay tribute in their desire for admission. What, then, are the privileges of legal marriage? They are material – the unit has advantages in state policy on personal taxation, social security benefits, national insurance, inheritance taxes. They are social – the unit is recognised and approved, it conforms to convention and experience. They are personal, in so far as legal marriage offers security, stability, the possibility of mutual financial obligation, rights of succession, claims on property on divorce. They are generational – the unit is medically and 'psy' approved for infer-tility treatment, adoption, parental rights on the break-up of relation-ships. It is suggested, however, that marriage is the model for intimate relationships because of its immortality and its status as icon. Whether it is invoked in political rhetoric or in religious ideology, marriage and family stand as a totem. Rationalistic questioning of function or privilege cannot remove emblematic status. This institution has to be understood in other contexts. Authority, patriarchal society, religion, politics, invoke the totem as a sacred source. Claiming to head the 'party of the family', Mrs Thatcher stated:

> There is no such thing as society. There are individual men and women and there are families. And no government can do anything except through people, and people must look to themselves first. A nation of free people will only continue to be great if family life continues and the structure of that nation is a family one. (*Woman's Own*, 31 October 1987: 10, quoted by Thomas, 1991)

Family rhetoric is understood. It calls on the primal and the sacred. Motherhood, sacrifice, caring for others, images of comfort, reassurance and stability. A place to go when one has nowhere else. But the images conjured up containing elements of personal experience combined with the immemorial, the unwritten, permits fluidity, unspecificity. Political rhetoric can manipulate this:

If we are to sustain, let alone extend, the level of care in the community, we must first put the responsibility back where it belongs, with the family and the people themselves. (Centre for Policy Studies, 1977: 83)

In this case 'family' and 'married women' are largely synonymous.

Marriage, State, Polis

As befits an ancient institution, marriage has its iconography. Symbols are: engagement ring, church announcements, public notices, invitations, special clothes, wedding dress, veil, prescribed colours, flowers, bouquet, attendants, witnesses, wedding ring, ritualistic words, ceremony, music, signature and record. Marriage is a *rite de passage* to be celebrated with food, wine, speech; to be recorded on film. Consider how a few bars of Mendlessohn's Wedding March can invoke immediate images and the power of institution and ritual is evident. Later, photographs in silver frames, engagement and wedding rings serve as reminders of changed legal status, and as sign to others.

The legal and the social are mixed in wedding ritual, as is the political. For marriage provides 'the basic unit of our society. It is within the family that the next generation is nurtured' (Thatcher, *The Times*, 17 October 1981). There is a kind of uniform monotony in our fates. We are destined to marry or to enter similar relationships. As Natalia Ginzburg (1985: 8) says: 'our lives unfold according to ancient, unchangeable laws, according to an invariable and ancient rhythm ... our life slips by'.

It is not just the wedding which is ritual, but the lived experience of marriage. It is a material condition, a visible structure of everyday life. Experienced as a system of images, confirmed by wedding and family pictures, re-enacted through anniversary custom, its traces are visible everywhere. Despite deconstructionist critique, perhaps because of its all-embracing but unspecific nature, marriage endures as symbol. The marriage order, like the legal order, is a matter of what is lived, accepted and made familiar, or family. It may be presented as private but it is reinforced everywhere in public and in political discourse. Marriage has its own rituals, children, coupledom, Saturday nights out, reunions, a familiar tradition learned and transmitted at home. It does not have to be rational, its origins are sacred, it can call on mythology, an unconscious reservoir of memories, emblems, a fictive narrative. In a sense, the problem for those excluded from legal marriage is that, despite logic and rationality which may be marshalled to support change, there is no reason to listen, and their voices may not be heard. Children carry forward the tradition, unwritten, custom. Marriage hallucinates in a repetition of ritual. It matters not that obedience is dropped from the marriage vow or that the ceremony takes place without a church. It invokes and evokes timeless, unspoken memory. It can resist theorising and theory. To break free from marriage as a timeless, unwritten institution whose terms are unequal and unjust has been the ambition of feminist writers. Legal theorists have deconstructed marriage to point up the gendered nature of its terms. Yet others find a solution in a freely negotiated contract to be agreed by the partners. Contract as the model of political relations and the justification of the state is presented as a solution to marriage difficulties, as a principle of social association, and as a means of creating social relationship, such as couple agreements. This is reinforced by pointing to entry into marriage as free and voluntary. Recent work on family and social contract raises doubts about this line of reasoning. In her powerful book *The Sexual Contract* (1988a) Carole Pateman criticises the limitations of social contract theory in justifying current political arrangements. The sexual contract, which predated the social contract, gave men conjugal mastery over women, realised through marriage. Readings of major social contract theorists from Hobbes to Rousseau confirm that the family is taken as natural, as pre-given. Marriage, the foundation of family, ensures the subordination of women, which is presented as inevitable. The free individuals who contract in the social contract are male. The issue of whether or not women contract freely into the sexual contract is unresolved, and the way out for political theorists is to tell patriarchal stories in which marriage and family are 'natural'.

Pateman likens the position of women in the sexual contract to that of the slave, much discussed in political theory. In marriage women give up autonomy over themselves in exchange for protection. But the obedient wife cannot enforce protection, although the protector can enforce obedience. The marriage contract is not like the employment contract because there is 'one fundamentally important difference between wives and other labourers. Only women become (house) wives and provide "domestic service" – even though all masters demand – service – from their subordinates' (1988a: 125). It is sometimes said that employers construct the employment contract on the assumption that there is a housewife to take care of the worker's daily needs. It is time that the inflexibility of employment contracts keeps mothers out of the labour market or limits their participation. Yet the husband does not contract for his wife's labour power, but for bodily servitude, more akin to that of the slave.

Although women are taking control of their sexuality and bodies, there remain contradictions surrounding women and contract in relation to political theory and to marriage. The positing of the family as 'natural', pre-dating the state, in political philosophy leaves unspecified social understanding of that unit. There can be no doubt that the fathers of social contract theory wrote in the context of subordination, at a time when married women could not contract, as their legal existence was subsumed under that of their husband. For Pateman the notion of the free, contracting citizen of the modern state remains tainted by its origins in male individualism and female subordination. We shall return to this in Chapter 6.

Marriage as contract provides other problems. As we have seen, the contract cannot be entered into by two or more adults but is restricted to two sexually ascriptive persons who cannot have similar contracts elsewhere; the parties cannot set the terms themselves, as that is done by law; the couple cannot fix the extent, duration or end of the contract; one party gives up bodily autonomy, awaiting the exercise of the male conjugal right to establish the contract; the contract does not exist as a written document which is read and then signed. It seems therefore that contract is an inappropriate word for marriage particularly since the duties therein are ascriptively determined in accordance with sex. Empirical studies confirm that child care and housework remain largely women's work. In Pateman's view:

> marriage and the patriarchal family are carried over into the new civil order. There is no need for the classic contract stories to include an account of the sexual contract. The original contract that creates civil society (which encompasses both the public and the private spheres) implicitly incorporates the sexual contract. In these stories, marriage and the patriarchal family appear as the natural, necessary foundation of civil life. (1988a: 110)

As the repressed story of political genesis is uncovered we may consider what else has been covered up. The notion of cover was deployed at law for seven centuries to account for the subordination of married women. As explained by Blackstone (1765), marriage makes the husband and wife one at law, the very legal existence of the wife being suspended, or at least incorporated, into that of the husband 'under whose wing, protection, and *cover*, she performs every thing', being called a feme covert and said to be 'covert-baron' under the influence of her husband/lord; 'and her condition during her marriage is called her coverture'. It is not surprising that feminist theorists argue that marriage, the polis, and civil society may be irreclaimable, as patriarchally conceived, instituted and constituted.

Old stories can retain a powerful hold. Stories affect the creation of law and its application. Such laws remain with us and mediate our perceptions of realities and truths. The stories influence what we see and what we can see. Our relationships with other human beings, at the centre of our lives, are structured by these ancient, unchangeable stories and laws. Dispelling their spell, taking up, uncovering what is hidden and what is silent, this work is just beginning.

5
Engendering Gender: Constructing Masculinity and Femininity

How do we make sense of that most basic feature of the family, roles differentiated according to gender? That this exists is part of our common understanding. Social scientific research has documented the allocation to women of child care and domestic responsibilities, something that is confirmed by casual observation. We understand that this is how things are. Shared knowledge of such family arrangements derives from our own experiences as children. And yet we also know of families where this is not so. Research, too, shows that the traditional nuclear family of breadwinner husband and dependent wife is an anachronism, unrepresentative of the majority of families. For in 1989 the majority of households in Britain did not conform to the typical pattern of a married couple with dependent children. Furthermore, in those households that did conform, the mother's participation in the workforce was likely to continue despite child-care responsibilities (*Social Trends*, 1991, Ch. 2). It seems we can hold on to the mythic image of tradition while simultaneously living in a very different way. How do we interpret this contradiction? What stories do we tell ourselves about gender and its meanings, about mothers and fathers? To what extent do we continue to uphold tradition as an ideal standard against which we judge – and pass or fail – ourselves and others?

Sex and gender are constructed in family law and its discourse. Indeed, the legal discourse of family cannot conceive of a person in whom gender is not a fundamentally determining attribute. This affects women and men, particularly those who deviate from the dominant paradigms of the feminine and masculine as constructed in law. For those acculturated to their appropriate role, this may involve a denial of self. There are a number of ways in which this can be discussed: textual, empirical, theoretical, experiential. Writing can be drawn upon from feminist theory, sociology, ethnomethodology, anthropology, economics and legal texts. There is a rich vein of work in this area, but it is largely confined to studies of women (Oakley, 1974; Wilson, 1977; Glendon, 1977, 1981; O'Donovan, 1979, 1985; Smart, 1984, 1989; Eaton, 1986; Burgoyne, Ormrod and Richards, 1987; Okin, 1989). Work on men is only just beginning (Seidler, 1989; Chapman and Rutherford, 1988; Segal, 1990). We have already seen how legal marriage insists on a sexual union of two biologically opposed persons. Law then expects them to conform to traditional roles incorporating or living out in their bodies normative modes of femininity and masculinity. The judges of gender normality are not confined to the courts; they are to be found in doctors' surgeries and hospitals, in adoption committees of social services departments, in education and corrective institutions, and in factories, plants and offices.

Despite efforts to use gender neutral language – removing specific references to men, women, husbands, wives, mothers, fathers, and instating spouses, parents and parties in their place – legal discourse has not escaped its transmission of gender normality. So long as legal marriage remains a central concept in family law, the gender message will continue to be transmitted. The heterosexual dyad is a union of opposites, a bi-polar model of attributes, bodies, gestures, conduct, aptitudes and expectations of what a gendered person is and what a gendered person does. The notion of parenthood is not gender neutral. In culture, in popular morality, in the juridical and 'psy' discourses, parents are mothers or fathers, with all that these distinct terms imply.

Ann Oakley (1974) in a pioneering study of the role of housewife argues that mother, father, wife and husband are distinct roles that could be performed on a non-gendered basis, but that this has not happened. The allocation to women of the role of housewife endures, even when both partners work outside the home. This leads to doubts about the possibility of change:

> The capacity of the housewife's employment to affect fundamentally and permanently the structure of marital roles is undermined by the ideology of non-interchangeability, of role segregation, subscribed to by the married couple – the ideology of gender differentiation which is basic to marriage as an institution.

Thus it is in the marriage (or marriage-type) relationship that the sexes are opposed and differentiated. For women the ideology of home and family remain as paramount in the 1990s as when Oakley was writing, as a recent survey shows. Only 9 per cent of mothers questioned said that they would put their career before their families (MORI, 1991, *Independent*, 21 September 1991). That the family has priority over women's employment, particularly when children are small, and that it is mothers who make the accommodation, was established in a major review (Martin and Roberts, 1984). It seems that gender roles are first observed and learned in the family. In the sense that they are internalised they are not imposed, and differentiation of male and female children occurs at a variety of levels in growing up, with males learning to distance themselves from their mother and her world. Law plays a part in confirming that this gender order is right and proper.

It is not just a matter of differentiation but also of hierarchy. Much research concentrates on the domestic and child-caring role of women, and on their subordination. The construction of men as superior in the hierarchy has received little attention. Elizabeth Wilson (1977) argues that the male role is constructed to reinforce the work ethic. The ability to support a family is identified with manhood in the male child's mind. Dependency of wife and children provide a male incentive to work, while virility is confirmed in the role of family head. Thus men are identified with paid employment, and women with domesticity, regardless of their personal reality. That this is how masculinity is perceived by many is confirmed in recent work (Seidler, 1989). Whether the fragmentation of identity, a feature of the late modern world, will affect these perceptions remains in question. Our purpose in this chapter is to investigate the extent to which law supports and reinforces the modern gender order.

One explanation for the identification of manhood with paid employment and the support of a family lies with the concept of the 'family wage', which developed in the nineteenth century in response to the demands of certain male craft unions. This coincided with the growth of an ideology of separate spheres for the sexes, and with an idealisation of domesticity (Pinchbeck, 1930: 312). This change had a dramatic effect on family ideology, the effects of which are still felt today. Notions of family life, masculinity, fatherhood, what it means to be a mother, femininity, have been constituted according to these familial values. Legal texts which confirm men in the workplace and women in the home can be found in legislation, regulations, court judgments. Other confirmatory sources are interviews with court and other legal officials, statements by politicians, social work policies on the family, studies of specific institutions. To this may be added studies of the 'psy' discourses and the construction therein of normality, particularly of concepts of masculinity and femininity. This material is so rich and varied that it is not possible to summarise it here. It permeates this text. To substantiate the point, however, we turn to legislative provisions and court pronouncements. This section concludes with an important study of the magistrate's court.

There was a time when it was a simple matter to point out the sexism of the law (Sachs and Wilson, 1978; Atkins and Hoggett, 1984; O'Donovan, 1979). In the recent past legislators have taken pains to draft laws in gender neutral terms; judges have been more careful about expressing their views – unlike the judge in 1982 in Cambridge Crown Court who said of a rape victim: 'If she does not want it, she has only to keep her legs shut' (*The Times*, 11 December 1982). To understand how gender is legally engendered we can consider, first, direct textual statements, but we should bear in mind that these are only part of the story. Statements by judges are part of the law, as are legislative provisions. But law is more than these specifics. Secondly, institutional gender provisions are discussed. These are reinforced by law in the economic and social organisation of life. Finally, an empirical study with theoretical underpinnings is introduced. It is the law's role in reinforcing existing material and ideological conditions which is under scrutiny. In other words, the relationship between law and the family is complex. Although law is a powerful force in continuing the story of traditional gender, it did not write the epic. Legislation in gender-specific terms remaining on the statute book can be found in family law – the Married Women's Property Act 1882, 1964; and in criminal law – the Infanticide Act 1938.

Is the elimination of gendered legislation, whether based on beliefs about biology or social role, a progressive step? Is the greater care to appear neutral now exercised by the judiciary a step forward? This chapter will argue that, despite a greater awareness whereby directly gendered provisions have been largely eliminated, institutional sexism, which is harder to identify and root out, remains. In any case, writers have argued that the more gender neutral law appears to be, the more 'ruthlessly male' it is (MacKinnon, 1987).

Family law is about women and men. In the standard legal paradigm marriage is between two persons 'respectively male and female' (Matrimonial Causes Act 1973, s. 11). This story is about a model of normality, which includes a sexual binary system. Family law is permeated with gender. It is not neutral. As Carol Smart (1984: 4) states: 'the law itself reproduces and perpetuates the most secure foundations of patriarchal relations, namely the family and gender divisions'. The use of the term 'patriarchal relations' signals that gender divisions are not neutral, but imbued with power relations and hierarchy. Smart's study of English family law from the 1950s establishes that the family is a 'collection of ideological cultural and economic factors, imbued with certain power relationships between family members and constantly idealised as the goal to which we should all aspire' (1984: 5).

Mary Eaton (1986) has undertaken a detailed study of a particular court in England at Magistrates' Court level. She finds a model of family life, constantly reiterated, which dominates discourse in the Magistrates' Court. In understanding gender hierarchy and how it is reproduced, examination of the subtle operation of this model is enlightening. In the course of her study of a specific Magistrates' Court (pseudonym Hillbury) Eaton became aware of a particular model of the family in pleas of mitigation on behalf of both women and men. This model of the family ascribes specific, differentiated, gender roles to women and men. The ideological dominance of this model is not matched by its empirical prevalence. Nevertheless the dominance of this model means that other forms of household arrangement are marginalised. In this model women are assumed to be 'primarily home-centred' (1986: 12), and the woman who conforms to this model receives more sympathy than the woman who does not. This is termed a 'chivalrous' response but, as Eaton points out, we should be sceptical about its benefits because the role identified is so restrictive. Pat Carlen (1987) confirms that resistance to the oppression of one's gender role makes one subject to the coercion of the penal system. Although the work discussed relates to women, the finding is probably also true of men. Further confirmation concerning the penal system can be found in Hilary Allen's research (1987) on criminology.

Part of this argument is that the ascribed gender role itself is a form of social control. Eaton's study confirms this. Married women get lower sentences for offences than do sole women. The more economically dependent a woman is on a man, the less formal control is recommended. Listening to a court rhetoric Eaton identified a voice: 'Children place a different complexion on it' (1986: 29, 30). Thus the family is depicted as a site for social responsibility. Lawyers go along with this, presenting defendants in appropriate gender terms, playing an 'appropriate social role', as a 'normal member of society'. Eaton's conclusion is that family roles are perceived by the court as a form of social control. Thus:

> Family circumstances are important in presenting both men and women to the court, but within the family, men and women are ascribed very different roles. The consequence for a woman of playing her traditional gender role within the family is a degree of unofficial but effective control which the courts seem to recognise when passing sentence. (1986: 30)

The model of the family identified is of a man engaged in paid employment and a woman involved in child care, both 'working for the family'. Spouses are viewed as guardians against further trouble, children as social responsibility. This basic unit is to be preserved, if possible. Although an instrument of social control, the family is also a privileged institution: 'behaviour which would have been reprehensible outside the context of the family is viewed differently when "family feelings" are involved' (1986: 62). However, privilege is extended only to those units which conform to the model of normality assumed by the court. It is not just the magistrates and lawyers who engage in familiar discourse, but also social workers and others attached to the courts.

Discussion of the construction of gender roles and identities must include the participation of social workers in familialist rhetoric. The part played by the probation service as court officers reinforces the dominant model of the family. Power of a quasi-juridical nature is exercised by social workers in the preparation of social inquiry reports for magistrates, in the assessment of children, in the supervision of 'problem' families, and in the assessment of prospective adopters. Confirmation of this role in relation to the probation service comes in a Home Office Circular (1971, no. 59, para 11) which identifies a task of the social inquiry report as an inquiry into '... the character, personality and social and domestic background of the accused'. Drawing up a report involves an endorsement or denial of the arrangements encountered in the defendant's family life. According to Eaton (1986) this assumes a model of appropriate family life involving the subordination of women, and the confirmation of men as breadwinners and dominant. She provides a series of telling examples.

Home visits, although made to both women and men, are structured according to gender: 'the pattern that emerges from the reports suggests that to learn more about a woman it is sufficient to visit her home, but to learn more about a man, one must see the individuals who share his home' (Eaton, 1986: 66). Visits to women resulted in descriptions of the home, with the domestic sphere seen as the prime responsibility of women, who are judged by the appearance of the home. Competence in the domestic sphere, or lack of it, and responsibility for child care was attributed to women. Of 12 visits to women, ten resulted in comments on standards of comfort and cleanliness within the home; of ten visits to men only four resulted in such comments, 'but even in these reports the man was not held responsible for the appearance of the home' (1986: 66), rather this was attributed to a woman. While women are judged by appearances, men are judged by the 'significant adult' in their lives, usually a woman. It seemed that meeting a female dependant was an important test of male stability and normality. Eaton's conclusion is that women are expected to account for themselves and their menfolk within the domestic sphere, the emotional situation there being their responsibility. Work and the support of dependants are a form of social control of men. The Magistrate's Court provides one example of the constitution of gender roles in quasi-juridical discourse. The model of the traditional nuclear family upheld is that prevailing elsewhere and reproduced culturally in the mass media, the education system, the labour market. It is hardly surprising to find courts endorsing the social structure from which they derive their authority.

Constructing Masculinity

However good a sort of man the husband may be, he could not perform the functions which a mother performs by nature in relation to a little girl. (*M* v. *M*, 1979: 92)

It is natural for young children to be with mothers but, where there is a dispute, it is a consideration not a presumption. (*Re S*, 1991: 390)

Being man, in legal discourse, means being certain attributes, a particular role. It is not just being active in penetrative sex, or being a breadwinner, but a complex set of abilities and limitations which are understood but generally left unspecified. For although it is often said that woman is defined against the male norm, that woman is 'the other', that woman is whatever man is not, an opposite in the discursive binary system which takes masculinity as normality and femininity as the blemished remains, we may inquire whether this is so in discourses surrounding the family. While resisting an unthinking notion of family it is nevertheless possible to identify it in popular speech, or in the mind of the 'reasonable man', as woman's domain. This makes the unwrapping of masculinities at home difficult. Men are supposed to be abroad, in the world; in familial discourse they are not familiar. They do not see themselves as gendered subjects. Because of their power, men do not have to define themselves in relation to women.

This section considers the sexed male as object of a discourse of normality and abnormality. Two areas present themselves: the construction of the normal male body as that of the potent heterosexual male, as illustrated by cases on nullity of marriage and divorce; and the treatment of homosexuality as a problem in family relations. This latter aspect will be dealt with in the section on stigmatised identities. The sexual division of labour provides a rich terrain for digging, as does the juridical discourse on the custody of children.

The Potent Heterosexual Male

Moran (1990) and Collier (1991b) argue that the law on consummation of marriage is one of the sites at which the male body was sexualised, and at which male heterosexual sexuality within the institution of marriage emerged. Moran (1990: 155) observes that male sexuality is presented as 'timeless, necessary, inevitable and exhaustive', but as open to question. Those with other experiences are silenced by the seeming naturalness of this discourse. In a specific consideration of the idea and practices of sexuality in male heterosexuality within the context of the family in law, he examines a series of cases of allegation of non-consummation of marriage because of the husband's impotence.

The discourse in *Welde* v. *Welde* (1731) concerning impotence spoke of 'absolutely and naturally incapable'; the act of generation; remedies to be granted for non-performance of conjugal duty. 'It is through the juridical requirements that a knowledge of the male body is produced' (Moran, 1990: 157). But in *Welde* the court remained sceptical as to proof of impotence, because the absolute incapacity was not visible: '"The surgeons returned, that he had all the parts of generation in due and proper proportion and that it did evidently appear to them he was capable to perform the act of generation"' (1731: 447, cited by Moran, 1990: 160). The wife was therefore ordered to return to cohabit with the husband until three years should have elapsed from the date of the marriage. A second case, over 100 years later took a more knowledgeable approach to the male body: in *N* v. *M* (1853) the absence of visible signs of impotence did not bar the conclusion of impotence 'as regards the said woman'. The language of the court indicates a claim to read the body; aspects that were previously invisible are now open to judicial comment, and knowledge of the body and of male sexuality has been created. For example, the court presumes that it is in the 'nature' of the male to have sexual intercourse 'where persons both competent cohabit together', and that failure to do so indicates impotence of the husband (1853: 1439, cited by Moran, 1990: 163). Male sexuality is established as naturally active, penetrative, as forming the identity of the male. A third case, *G* v. *M* (1885), marks the emergence of the impotent male as a personage, in answer to the question 'what is he by nature?'. Such a personage can exist even without visible signs. In other words, a medico-legal discourse has been constructed which knows the truth of a male body, better than the owner of the body does himself. As Moran (1990: 170) observes: 'In *N* v. *M*, through the deployment of this new knowledge of the body, impotence becomes nature gone wrong. By the time *G* v. *M* comes before the court impotence is a pathological state, the key to a man's constitution, his character.'

Collier (1991b) details the construction of heterosexuality in legal discourse, arguing that 'the heterogeneous dimensions of the categories of masculinity and heterosexuality are each negated through a naturalist ideology which constructs masculinity and heterosexuality on the basis of essentialist presuppositions' (1991: 3). Representations of sexuality in law are significant ways of knowing and experiencing self and society, and in articulating individual subjectivity. In this, law links to cultural understandings of sexuality. Collier isolates five elements of sexual intercourse in law. These are: that sex is natural; that what is natural is heterosexual; that genital sex is primary; that 'true' sexual intercourse is phallocentric; that sex is something which takes place in marriage.

The particular construction of sexuality involves a clear definition of male heterosexual activity, and not only as natural but as definitive of the masculine. The penis is primary. It must be erect; it must penetrate; it must ejaculate. Impotence, the 'very antithesis of male virility' (Collier, 1991b), provides a clue to the judicial thinking about masculinity. If, culturally, 'sex' is often equated with 'intercourse' then impotence negates this sexual ideal. In relation to masculinity this is perhaps all the more important when 'genital sexuality has been identified as a mainstay of male gender identity and phallocentric culture' (1991b: 13).

It is Collier's argument that male sexual pleasure is central to the process of defining sexual intercourse, and that this is to be derived primarily through the act of penetration. For example, ejaculation in the vagina is not considered essential to consummation (*White* v. *White,* 1948). The inability to penetrate is unmanly, and such a charge is:

> a grave and wounding imputation that the respondent is lacking ... in the power of reproducing his species, a power which is commonly and rightly considered to be the most characteristic quality of manhood. (*C* v. *C,* 1991)

The point is that masculinity is equated with a particular form of penetrative sexuality; men who do not, or cannot, express their sexuality in this way are to be pitied, but are also guilty of a 'cruel wrong' (*G* v. *M,* 1885: 202); male instigation and initiation of sexual activity is presumed and advocated (*S* v. *S,* 1945); the search for psychological and physical techniques to promote virility have been judicially encouraged (*R.E.L.* v. *R.E.L.,* 1948); where the problem is one of vaginal blockage, the virile man is expected to attempt to keep trying. What emerges from this is the judicial picture of normal male sexuality. As Collier (1991b: 26) points out, the 'representations of potent masculinity which emerge from the above cases are deeply phallocentric'.

The normal male does not talk about his feelings, or about emotion in general. He is expected to be 'strong and silent'. This may be taken into account, judicially, in order to compensate the uncommunicative male for unspoken hurts he is taken to be suffering silently. In *Ralevski* v. *Dimovski* (1986, cited by Grbich, 1991: 74) the male plaintiff/appellant suffering a cosmetic injury initially disclaimed any embarrassment about the scars on his face. The appeal court was 'inclined to believe that the initial answer did not represent a true indication of the appellant's feelings but a response to perceived norms of a culture which is inclined in some quarters to deny males the luxury of the public admission of concern about their appearance'. Thus, despite aspirations to gender neutrality, the gender of the individual before the court is a relevant factor.

The Sexual Division of Labour

Gender is a total social fact in the classic Maussian sense of the term:

> in these *total* social phenomena, as we propose to call them, all kinds of institutions find simultaneous expression: religious, legal, moral and economic. In addition, the phenomena have their aesthetic aspect ... (Mauss, 1954: 2)

What we are all engaged in is the performance of our gender roles and we must establish our gender credentials in the projection of selves. Consider how we do so. We receive help from those around us who order their perceptions and interpretations according to the expectation that people should fall into one of two gender categories. The perceived 'naturalness' of gender dichotomy and membership of one or other category ignores the extent to which gender is socially and culturally achieved. Prescriptions as to behaviour follow from ascriptive categorisation. From these follow the sexual division of labour. Thus, Patrick Jenkin, then Secretary of State for Social Services said:

> Quite frankly, I don't think that mothers have the same right to work that fathers do. If the good Lord had intended us to have equal rights to go out to work, he wouldn't have created man and woman. These are biological facts. (*Man Alive*, BBC, 1979)

But the consequences of the 'work privilege' for men is that they are not seen as suitable for taking care of children.

The imposition on men of the breadwinning role does not always correspond to the ways in which lives are lived. But it does generally result in the exemption of men from housework and child care if there is a woman available to take on these tasks. The identification of men with wage earning, of their well-being with material possessions and the ability to provide for a family, leads to an instrumentality with regard to self. Living in order to work, denying needs and emotion, men are constantly on their guard against others, establishing their self-esteem through independence and self-sufficiency, according to Seidler (1988). This denial of aspects of self, of dependence and emotional needs, is based on an association of masculinity with control: autonomy, mastery of oneself and one's environment. For these reasons, and as paid work gives a sense of control over one's life, few men are legally able, or are prepared, to take time off in relation to paternity, a sick child, and other parental responsibilities such as visits to doctor or dentist. The prescriptions of juridical and 'psy' discourses become prescriptions for self.

Where men do give up paid work in order to undertake child care, this is not judicially approved:

> I find it very hard, with children of this age, to think, unless there is some real criticism of the mother's ability as a mother, it is right and in the best interests of these little children that they should be cut off from her ... [and] the father will have to give up his work ... it is a totally artificial situation to bring about to have a father giving up his work, which is his career and will certainly be something which he will need to follow for the rest of his working life, to live

on social security to look after two small children when the mother is fully available to look after them.

... The result [of the previous court order] cannot be said to be in the long-term interest of these children. It cannot be to their interest to have a father who is not working. (*Plant* v. *Plant*, 1983)

This suggests that the judiciary internalise prescriptions about gender roles which they then prescribe for other men. The transcript of the trial in *B* v. *B* (1985), a child-custody case, show how the judge insisted on paid work as a necessary aspect of being male.

I shall take a great deal of convincing that it is right that an adult male should be permanently unemployed in order to look after one small boy. I am sure you will address your mind to that. (Judge to father's lawyer, p 173)

The judge addressed a number of direct questions to the father (who was the primary child carer) about his intention to get a job and the inquiries he had made.

Obviously, as I am sure you appreciate, a healthy young man like you must generate resources by your work to support your child and yourself – certainly as a minimum, these two – rather than having other people supporting you through the tax payer. (*B* v. *B*, 1985)

Further questions were asked about apprenticeship, qualifications, previous employment and how the father would manage now his son was about to start school.

When the court welfare officer gave evidence the following exchange took place:

Judge: Employment for the father is going to introduce all sorts of possible complications.

Welfare Officer: Oh yes ... I would presume that in the case of Mrs B [mother] she would not necessarily be faced with that situation. She would probably wait until the child was well established at school and try to commit her time with it. It is much easier possibly for a woman than for a man (*B* v. *B*, 1985: 176–77).

In his judgment (which was later reversed by the Court of Appeal) the judge emphasised that the 'father's primary role must be by his work to generate resources which provide for the support and maintenance of his child and himself' (*B* v. *B*, 1985: 177). This was not just common sense, or the public interest in terms of the taxpayer, but it: 'is taking account of the child's interests. A son particularly looks to his father for example and pattern ... that of a working, earning and supporting father' (*B* v. *B*, 1985: 178).

The Court of Appeal (1985) agreed that the work role of the male is important and that the father's employment is a relevant consideration, but pointed out that the welfare of the child was best served by a continuation of the arrangement whereby the father had custody.

Within marriage-type relationships there are clear judicial ideas of an appropriate division of labour. Thus Lord Denning was surprised at the physical work undertaken by the plaintiff in *Cooke* v. *Head* (1972):

> She used a sledge hammer to demolish some old buildings. She filled the wheelbarrow with rubble and hard core and wheeled it up the bank. She worked the cement mixer, which was out of order and difficult to work. She did painting and so forth. The plaintiff did much more than most women would do.

Evidently, this work should have been done by the man. However, having behaved like a man the plaintiff was rewarded as one and received a share of the proceeds of the property involved. Similarly, in *Eves* v. *Eves* (1975), the plaintiff's active role was commented upon, including stripping wallpaper, painting inside and out, breaking up concrete, carrying concrete to a skip, demolishing one shed and putting up another, preparing the front garden for turfing. Again, these activities are described as more appropriate to a male.

It is evident that masculine culture contains understandings of the world and of the male place in it – 'Try to imagine how it feels to grow up believing that you have to be prepared to fight to prove yourself a man' is a piece of advice given to those who doubt this. Not all men participate in one unitary masculine culture; there are class, regional, ethnic variations. But until recently military service was compulsory for young men, and conscription into the armed forces at times of war remains a possibility. In the study of a Yorkshire mining village, *Coal Is Our Life* (Dennish et al., 1969), men and women are revealed to have separate lives, almost secret from one another, when married: 'For the husband to maintain his status and prestige in his social life with his peers, he must consciously distance himself from his wife and children, and be seen to do so' (1969: 75). This suppression of affection and desire is accompanied by a social construction in which only a 'real man' can become a miner. Husbands have greater freedom and power than wives, the latter being charged with home and hearth. Even where mines are closed, and husbands are no longer breadwinners, this social construction continues to be upheld in a cultural comprehension of honour and pride.

It may be objected that men are no longer sole, or even primary, breadwinners and that the foregoing analysis is outdated. Women's participation in the labour market of the late twentieth century is a market feature, and their desire for greater participation has been documented (Martin and Roberts, 1984: 19). Pointing to this, however, does not dispel implicit cultural understandings and internalisation of gender norms by men and women. It may be that prescriptions about man's place in the market or woman's in the home have been undermined, but a gendered division of labour in the family and in the market continues.

Paternal Custody Claims

Decisions on the future residence of children, if brought to court, are made on the legal authority of legislation which is gender neutral (Matrimonial Causes Act 1973; Children Act 1989). In about 94 per cent of divorces involving children there is no court dispute. Whether by agreement of the parents or in default of such, children tend to live with the parent who wants to have them. In the overwhelming majority of cases this is the mother. This is so marked a feature of Anglo-Welsh society that the extraterrestrial visitor might perceive a legal rule on maternal preference. No such legal rule exists in formal terms. The hypothesis advanced is that this custom is based on a gender rule. Fair enough, the reader may reply, since mothers undertake most of the pre-divorce child care. What we have is a social rule whereby the primary child carer continues in that role after a parental parting. However, one cannot go further and assert that this has nothing to do with gender.

It is fair to suggest that gender roles in parenting and in the labour market construct men in such a way that they are unlikely to seek the care of their children after a divorce. Although academic commentators emphasise the neutrality of the legislation, they tend to omit the gendered base on which it operates. An exception is Richards (1982) who accounts for the fact that in only a small percentage of cases do the children live with the father after divorce:

> In most cases the father has not sought custody and does not challenge his wife's claim. The main reason for this situation is that the general assumptions that are held about the sexual division of labour within marriage are extended to the post-divorce situation.

Descriptive as the words 'sexual division of labour' are, they fail to bring out the self-definition involved: what it means to be a 'real man' or a 'good father'.

According to the study by Eekelaar et al. (1977), only 6 per cent of cases in their major study of custody after divorce were contested in court. Although the courts did not favour either sex as the most suitable custodian, but rather 'minimum disruption to the child's existing emotional ties' (para. 13.20), nevertheless mothers were much more likely to have such ties and therefore to win.

Although the welfare principle is the basis for decision, it should not be overlooked that in justifying a choice between competing parents the judiciary is engaged in moral discourse. There are four aspects to this: child centredness; judgement of the past; normative models of gendered behaviour; and relational morality. Although the decision may be couched in a language of the welfare, or the best interests, of the child, there is an implicit moralising involved. One parent is said to be better able to serve the child's needs. Despite the child centredness of the language, the decision also judges the past and predicts future behaviour. But the language is normative to further degree: it lays down that men are more suitably engaged in economic activities than in child care, whereas the opposite is true of women. Finally, mothers are assessed as possessing those qualities of warmth and understanding deemed necessary for child rearing. This last aspect, termed 'relational morality', will be further discussed below. It is not here being asserted that gender is irrelevant to decisions concerning the best person to bring up a child where parents cannot decide together. Gender has to be understood in its present and past context. The purpose is to deconstruct the representations of gender which appear in legal texts.

We can isolate attributes of parenting and masculinity, as traditionally understood. The good father is a good provider and therefore a breadwinner whose place is in the market rather than at home. In *A* v. *A* (1988) the trial judge commented that it was a father's role to go out to work to support his children. On appeal the court said that there was 'no legal presumption that a mother should have the custody of young children', nevertheless the judge could not be faulted if he was 'moved to attach importance to the natural bond between mothers and young children' (*A* v. *A*, 1988: 58). Fathers are perceived as specialists in paid work and discipline and mothers as specialists in affection:

> It is perhaps this [discipline] which is typically the paternal aspect of parenting, just as much as intimate warmth and intimate care are typically the maternal aspect of parenting ... children who must be deprived by their parents' separation usually suffer the least if left to the care of the mother ... (*Re K (Minors)*, 1977)

If a father breaks out of the stereotype and makes 'an extremely good job of bringing up and looking after A [a small child] on his own since he has been at home all day' he may find that he is criticised (*B* v. *B*, 1985). The pursuit of remunerative employment is construed as a male duty to family and society. The dilemma for fathers is, as summed up by the Court of Appeal (*B* v. *B*, 1985: 177):

A father who does not take employment to the limit of his proper capacity is not fit to care for his child; the father who does take employment is unable to care for his child.

But while the Court of Appeal disapproved this construction which placed public policy of a male duty to work above the welfare of a child, nevertheless the Court took the view that, if the considerations concerning the parents were equally balanced, mothers should get custody. In other words, mothers are primary child carers and it is for fathers to support that through wage earning, whether living with that family unit or not.

However, a father who can provide a 'mother-figure' in his home for the children does not suffer the disadvantages of a father on his own. In *Re C (Minors)* (1978: 239) the choice was between the plaintiff stepfather's home where the children had lived for some years and the biological father's home with his new wife. The court preferred the latter, describing the stepfather as lacking 'female assistance'. Referring to the stepfather's home the court said:

> there is no visible mother-substitute for these children at the time when they badly need one. The aunt and the grandmother ... cannot take one any close day-to-day role in looking after these children, and so some woman would have to be found.

By comparison, the father's home conformed with conventional ideas about the appropriate base for child rearing.

> On the other hand, the father has a wife, a new wife, though it is true, a very young woman to take on so great a responsibility, but he has got a wife and a home which is a two parent home of an established kind.

These points add up to a prescriptive conventional masculinity. Added to this is the threat posed by homosexual, transsexual and transvestite fathers, as perceived through court cases below. But as recent work on masculinity shows, judicial views and popular opinion of what it is to be a man largely coincide (Chapman and Rutherford, 1988; Segal, 1990). Although the putative 'reasonable man' as the spokesman for convention does not figure in custody disputes, being replaced by the notion of the welfare of the child, nevertheless his presence is felt. It is hardly surprising then to find that men are less tenacious in seeking the company of their children than are women. Despite representations of a 'new man' actively involved with his children, the traditional model of masculinity holds sway.

According to the latest statistics on families in Britain (*Social Trends*, 1991: 38) the proportion of all families with dependent children which are lone-parent families has increased from 8 per cent in 1971 to 14 per cent in 1987. Of these, 12.3 per cent are headed by women. In other words, only 1.7 per cent are headed by men. These lone-parented families constitute 5.8 per cent of all households in Britain. These statistics confirm the gendered nature of child rearing. The proportions of lone mothers who are single, separated or divorced form 90 per cent of all lone mothers. Of these the majority are divorced.

Constructing Femininity

The culturally structured system we designate by the term 'gender' bears some relationship to the biological difference between women and men but is not reducible to it. Gender in daily social life is produced and reproduced as a Maussian 'total social fact'. Although the aesthetic, presentational and behavioral aspects are immediately evident, and often construed as 'natural', Mauss reminds us of institutional aspects, of which law is one. Femininity is constructed in legal discourse around the family as tenderness and warmth with children, as economic dependence on men, as physical need of protection against male violence. In law making politicians use similar language. Women who do not fit easily into a construction of feminine frailty, whether because of the way they live or because of their rejection of this constructed role, are condemned. However, it is understood that feminine frailty may lead to bitterness on the part of the woman scorned by a man. This construction is illustrated from legal materials on child custody and from political debate on divorce law.

Custody of Children
The idea that mothers have qualities which make them more suitable than fathers for the care of young children is embedded in social and judicial attitudes. Mothers are expected to mould their economic activities to fit in with child care, with the latter having priority. Thus, in an exchange in Parliament in 1967, Mr Pardoe challenged as follows: 'Is he saying that he believes it right and proper that married women with young children should go out to work?' Dr Gray: 'I would agree with the implicit criticism that it is better if the mother can stay at home' (Hansard, HC 1967–68, vol 758, col 830). The reiteration of this convention was greeted with general approval, and the empirical evidence is that most women internalise a norm, in that they put their families first (Martin and Roberts, 1984, Ch. 12). That is not to say that women with children do not engage in paid employment. On the contrary, not only are their earnings a significant part of the family

economy, but mothers will increase their time in paid work if arrangements can be made for child care.

Having primary responsibility for children means that women are construed in judicial discourse as having qualities of warmth which fit them for the role of child carer. The word 'natural' is often used to cover this belief. Thus, the New South Wales Supreme Court expressed this in terms of 'the common knowledge possessed by all citizens of the ordinary human nature of mothers ... the strong natural bond which exists between mother and child ... which ... expresses itself in an unrelenting and self-sacrificing fondness which is greatly to the child's advantage' (*Epperson* v. *Dampney*, 1976: 241). Similar language can be found in judgments in common law jurisdictions, sharing the English law tradition of looking to the welfare of the child. Thus, an English judge stated that the mother 'not as a matter of law but in the ordinary courses of nature, is the right person to have charge of young children' (*Re K (Minors)*, 1977). Research on masculinity confirms that women are seen as specialists in the emotional life whereas men specialise in autonomy and control (Chapman and Rutherford, 1988). However, the supposed essential connection between women's nature and empathy or masculinity and emotional distance is denied in writing which argues that this is socially and historically constructed rather than ontologically fixed (Seidler, 1988).

It is not the purpose here to enter into debates about joint custody, the privileging of one gender over the other in child-custody disputes, or changes in recent legislation. There are other sources for these debates (Smart and Sevenhuijsen, 1989; Bainham 1990). Rather, the purpose here is to show how notions of woman, of femininity, are constructed in juridical discourse. Where a woman does not conform to assumptions about the primacy of the home for her she may lose custody of her children. Not being a 'good mother' as demonstrated by leaving one's children may result in loss of them or in loss of a share of family assets on divorce.

The reasons for departure are relevant. Leaving because of a violent partner receives more sympathy than leaving to live with another man. Being ambitious in one's career, something opposed to femininity and maternity in this discourse, is to risk losing custody of children in a dispute. Graycar (1989: 165) cites an Australian example where the judge made clear his disapproval of the mother's

tendency to allow herself to be so absorbed by her personal ambitions as to show a lack of maternal feelings towards the children and to be unconscious of and unsympathetic to their emotional needs. (*Harrington* v. *Hynes*, 1982: 297)

The defendant was and still is a working mother. Prior to and at the time of the previous hearing she was enthusiastically pursuing a career which placed a strain on her ability to cope with the demands of her domestic life and her children. (*Harrington* v. *Hynes,* 1982: 302)

According to Graycar, Australian Family Court judges look for a substitute mother figure where both partners are full-time workers. Children are construed as needing attention and warmth, best provided by a woman. A father who can provide such a mother substitute is at an advantage. In other words, a full-time working mother lacks the qualifications of a 'real mother'.

Feminist writing on women and custody depicts women as primary child carers, whether in or out of paid work. Autonomous motherhood is presented as a desirable goal in this discourse, but mothers who deviate from conventional models of a 'good mother' are seen as victims of accusations of selfishness, immaturity, being a bad mother. For example, Smart (1989b: 19) expresses fears that 'the enhancement of father's rights will increase their control over women'. Although it is couched in essentialist terms, Smart's point seems to be that as the notion of motherhood is narrowly constructed in a particular form, non-conformists will have to conform or risk loss of custody. Conformity includes acknowledgement of male authority.

Divorce Debates

Current divorce law, enshrined in the Matrimonial Causes Act 1973 (MCA) is the product of debates in Parliament in 1967–68 which resulted in the Divorce Reform Act 1969. This was an attempt to give greater autonomy to partners to end their marriages. Where a couple has been separated for two years and agrees to divorce the parties may do so by consent (MCA 1973, s. 1 (2) (d)). Where a couple has been separated for five years one party may be granted a divorce without the consent of the other provided certain conditions are met (MCA 1973, s. 1 (2) (e)). The Act also contains three grounds based on fault: adultery, unreasonable behaviour and desertion (MCA 1973, s. 1 (2)). The debate in Parliament was particularly concerned with the innocent wife divorced against her will, probably under the five-year provision. Security for wives was seen as tied to the status of wife that had previously been guaranteed so long as there was 'good behaviour' and conformity to role (Hansard, 1967–68, vol 758, col 833). But wives were also accepted as vulnerable, as susceptible to having their lives ruined by divorce and ending up destitute (1967–68, vol 758, col 838). The stereotypes of ageing, dependent, faithful, deserted wife, of irresponsible husband susceptible to the attractions of a younger, predatory woman, and of bitter, spiteful first wife who refuses to divorce a man who has founded a second family, stalk the pages of Hansard.

'Most of us know that the charms and attractions of many women grow a great deal greater. However, in other cases they indisputably diminish' (*Hansard*, 1967–68, vol 758, col 833). Women are construed in terms of getting and holding a husband. But the 'totally innocent wife, who has never done the slightest harm, could be thrown over' (1968–69, vol 784, col 1956) and divorced against her wish, if the new bill became law. The picture painted is of a woman 'getting on in years and whose attractions are not as great as they were previously' (1967–68, vol 758, col 891) who is vulnerable financially, being middle aged, likely to 'find it extremely difficult to turn to, to learn a job and keep it at a time when her energies are not at their peak' (1968-69, vol 784, col 1956); vulnerable socially because of 'a poor expectation of remarriage' (1967–68, vol 758, col 897). Therefore, the provision permitting unilateral divorce after five years of living separately was labelled a 'Casanova's Charter'.

The fear that abandonment of the fault principle and the introduction of divorce against the wish of a faultless spouse would be an injustice to women has proved largely unfounded. At the report stage of the bill a letter to *The Times* (27 January 1968) from Mr G.H. Crispin QC was quoted:

> My experience satisfies me that the vast majority of petitioners will be men: that women who have committed no other offence than giving up a career, growing older and bearing and bringing up children, will be 'put asunder' against their wish if this bill ever becomes law.

But this prophecy has proved false. In 1971, 67,000 petitions for divorce were filed by wives, compared to 44,000 filed by husbands. In 1981, 123,000 were filed by wives, compared to 47,000 by husbands. In 1989 the figures were: for wives, 135,000; for husbands, 50,000 (*Social Trends*, 1991: 2.13). It is true that in 1971 40 per cent of decrees granted to husbands were on the 'fact' of five-year separation without consent. So we may conclude that a backlog existed. This 'fact' was also used in 27 per cent of decrees to wives. In 1989 about 5 per cent of decrees to wives were based on the five-year 'fact' compared to about 10 per cent to husbands (*Social Trends*, 1991: 2.15).

The divorcing husband, a middle-aged Casanova, was constructed as a 'butterfly flitting from flower to flower' (*Hansard*, 1967–68, vol 758, col 884). Men desert, women are ditched. If the wife wants to keep the husband he 'will slosh her about until she does divorce him' (1967–68, vol 758, col 881). Mr Casanova is susceptible to 'the attractions of another woman, untrammelled by domestic care and, in some cases, with no care in the world except how she can catch him' (1967–68, vol 758, col 838). Such women are determined to 'snaffle men of this type' with large incomes, men who go from wife to wife, serial monogamists (1967–68, vol 758, col 875). But not all second wives are calculating husband thieves; some wait many, many years in order to marry, meanwhile sewing on buttons, cooking meals and nursing her man when ill, just like 'the faithful wife' (1967–68, vol 758, col 858).

The bitter first wife who refuses to give her husband a divorce out of spiteful or mercenary motives also appears in this scenario. She too deserves sympathy when facing the neighbours and saying 'one's husband has walked out, when it gets round that one has been deserted for the younger woman or the prettier woman or the more attractive prospect' for 'it is then that one is really hurt and feels bitter' (1967–68, vol 758, col 1119). One member of the House of Lords quoted Congreve on hell having no 'fury like a woman scorned' (1968, vol 303, col 394).

The point of disinterring these speeches is to show the stereotypes, familiar to all of us from film and fiction. Although based on myth, the stereotypes retain their power and reappear when legislation affecting the family is debated. The language used in the debate also represents a claim on the part of legislators to know about the lives of those governed by law. The great majority of parliamentarians are male yet their claim to knowledge is not confined to personal experience or to a male standpoint. Rather, they purport to understand female psychology, to speak for women, whether innocent or bitter, husband snatching or abandoned. It is not just that subsequent information on divorce reveals the parliamentary pre-conceptions as mythic and wrong; it is the claim to know which must be subjected to scrutiny.

Stigmatised Identities

Persons who cannot account for their identities in conventional terms are socially stigmatised. This applies to origins, sexuality, gender, reproduction, work roles. Perhaps this is because such people are considered a threat, or because they reveal how other identities are carefully constructed (Garfinkel, 1967). We are all engaged in lifelong projects of identity construction; those who pass as normal can contrast themselves to the stigmatised. The strategies used by those with a stigma to be accepted reveal a lot about what it means to be 'normal'. Since the term 'passing' carries the connotation of being accepted as something one is not, it might not seem appropriate to the normal. But the purpose of its use here is to draw attention to the extent to which being normal is a 'contingent and practical accomplishment' (Garfinkel, 1967: 181). To pass as normal we must have some notion of what that means, of how to do it. The methods used are similar whether a biological male is passing as masculine or as feminine. What seems normal is an achievement.

Cultural values and social structures, often referred to as convention, may be relied on by people to ensure their sense of self. They may also be relied on by the powerful to retain their position in a hierarchy of identities. There are two questions of power here: the power to define what is normal and what is not; and the power to order a hierarchy among the normal and the stigmatised.

What are we engaged upon as we project our gender identities? How does gender attribution actually work and how do we participate? Transsexuals and homosexuals are treated by legal and social practices as persons with stigmatised gender identities. In so doing law and society send messages about the 'natural, the normal'. The discourse about normality is not just the standpoints of individuals, however constructed, nor is it limited to institutional structures which produce and reproduce the experience of everyday life, but it must be extended to claims to knowledge. In the discussion of the potent heterosexual male we saw how knowledge of the male body is produced in juridical discourse. Because of claims to truth made by that discourse, and because law has the power to claim truth, knowledge produced by juridical discourse has high status among competing knowledge. It must be so if legislation or the judge says so. Law's power to claim truth is discursive but also coercive. According to Foucault (1988: 132), 'truth' refers to 'the ensemble of rules according to which the true and the false are separated and specific effects of power attached to the true'. This knowledge, this truth, permits the construction of the normal and the abnormal. Those constituted abnormal have stigmatised identities.

Feminist legal theorists have challenged law's claim to know about, to construct, women. Women's accounts of experiences, it is said, are ignored or constituted inexpert, irrational, unscientific, illogical, unreasonable or merely gossip. By contrast, mainstream theories of law are representations from the male point of view, from 'the male experience of power' (Grbich, 1991: 65). Experiences provide one means of challenging the authenticity or truth of constructions contained in law. However, it is not claimed that women or those with stigmatised identities share viewpoints, or have some special claim to truth. Rather, the point is to challenge the universality of constructions of normality, of claims to knowledge and truth.

The stigmatised identities of transsexual or homosexual are represented in family law directly by a denial of the right to marry and found a family. These identities are directly subject to criminal law under the Sexual Offences Act 1967. Indirectly stigmatised persons are subjects of juridical and 'psy' discourses which deny their suitability as child carers or adopters. Ideas about normality are translated into law, but also affect discourses about the welfare of children and about suitable parents and homes for their upbringing. A significant method of constructing, reconstructing and perpetuating the normal is through use of a language of binary oppositions. Categories are created in contrast to one another, and adjectives or adverbs are used for the attributes belonging to each category. Thus fathers discipline and mothers give affection.

Male Homosexuality

It is argued by Foucault (1981) that, prior to the late nineteenth century, male homosexuality was a variant of sexuality, but that the emergence of a discourse of perversity created a particular kind of male, the homosexual, a personage outwith the law:

> There is no question that the appearance in nineteenth century psychiatry, jurisprudence and literature of a whole series of discourses on the species and subspecies of homosexuality, inversion, pederasty and 'psychic hermaphrodism' made possible a strong advance of social controls into this area of 'perversity'. (Foucault, 1981: 101)

Homosexuality as a peculiar category was created around the 1870s. There were changes also, according to Collier (1991b), in definitions of sexuality, childhood and family relations. Just as a medico-legal discourse of knowledge of the male body developed, so too did noting of normality and abnormality. The homosexual, as personage, was placed firmly in the latter category.

Homosexual acts between consenting males aged 21 or over, in private, have been decriminalised (Sexual Offences Act 1967). But homosexual relationships are denied legitimacy. Denied that formal recognition available in Denmark (see Chapter 3), they are to be discouraged (Local Government Act 1988, s. 28). As Digby Anderson, government advisor, wrote in a letter to *The Times,* such alternatives to the heterosexual family are perceived as a threat to official policy: 'Society depends on the institution of the family for the care of both children and the elderly and the maintenance of values. It cannot let that institution be relativised away as one of a number of optional lifestyles' (*The Times*, 3 February 1988). Broadening the concept of 'family' is not considered in this letter, nor is the possibility that care of others may occur outside traditional relationships.

Male homosexuality tells us something about masculinity, the male and his anxieties. Being 'soft' or 'wet' are terms of abuse applied to men. We learn to identify masculinity with certain traits and behaviour. The hero is presented as the autonomous stranger, outside the everyday ties and responsibilities of family. Being dominant is being male; yet gentleness and patience in loving relationships are also commended. The inconsistencies create anxieties. Homophobia may create a self-hatred in homosexuals unable to conform to the masculine ideal 'a fatal flaw in masculinity' according to Quentin Crisp (1968) or a 'crippled state of being' (Gould, 1983: 99).

Homosexuals cannot marry a partner of the same sex, as discussed in Chapter 3. Child custody and visitation applications bring out the judicial attitudes to homosexuality and the categorisation of abnormality. In the case of men, very few cases concern a claim to have the child living with a homosexual father. *Re D* (1977) provides an example where the House of Lords, faced with an appeal of an application to adopt by the mother and her new husband, declared that:

Whatever new attitudes Parliament or public tolerance may have chosen to take as regards the behaviour of consenting adults over 21, *inter se*, these should not entitle the courts to relax, in any degree, the vigilance and severity with which they should regard the risk of children, at critical ages being exposed or introduced to ways of life which, as this case illustrates may lead to severance from normal society, to psychological stresses and unhappiness and possibly even to physical experiences which may scar them for life.

Although the father sought only to visit his child the court used putative common sense against him. It was suggested that 'a reasonable man would say "I must protect my boy, even if it means parting with him forever, so that he can be free from this danger"' (*Re D,* 1977). The father had said to the trial judge that he did not think it right that his son should be subjected to homosexual influences and that he could guarantee that such would not be the case. This evidence of internalisation of social fears of homosexuality did not convince the judge, who considered the father's influence likely to be harmful. The Court of Appeal reversed holding that the father's objections to adoption were to be judged not by the standard of the 'reasonable man', but by the standards of the hypothetical reasonable homosexual father. The House of Lords restored the trial judgment, saying that the reasonable parent 'would inevitably want to protect his boy from these dangers, that this parent, to his credit recognised this, and the trial judge so decided'.

Deconstructing fears of judiciary, social workers or other powerful persons concerning homosexual parents reveals explicit and implicit anxieties. Crane (1982, ch. 7) identifies four aspects: concern about social stigmatisation of the child; fears that the child will grow up homosexual or confused about his/her sexuality; a belief that a heterosexual household is preferable to a homosexual household as a child's home; fear that 'alternative lifestyles' undermine the 'normal' heterosexual family. As can be deduced, these fears operate at a number of levels: the immediate external environment of school and friends; the internal environment in the home; the child socialisation process; general social policy.

In a major article on homosexuality and child custody, Bradley (1987) identifies eleven cases subsequent to *Re D*. These concern both mothers and fathers whose sexual preferences are presented as problematic in relation to their wishes to live with their children or to see them regularly. However, it is conceded that information about judicial decisions in this area may be limited. In relation to the twelve decisions reviewed, Bradley (1987: 189) sees judicial pragmatism in determining the welfare of the children involved. In particular, the majority of the judges were cautious about expressing gratuitous personal opinions on the morality of homosexuality. Nevertheless 'descriptions of a homosexual way of life as "odd", "unusual and irregular" or "rather extraordinary" were not unusual' (1987: 189).

Pragmatic considerations do play a part and much depends on the circumstances of each parent. A home with an 'unusual' parent is better than none. However, this writer wishes to advance the hypothesis that a homosexual father is seen as more threatening to his children, and to society in general, than a lesbian mother. The explanation offered refers back to discussion of constructions of masculinity and femininity earlier in this chapter. For this reason lesbian motherhood will be dealt with below.

In *Re G* (1980) a homosexual father whose two daughters knew of his existence despite lack of contact applied to see them on a regular basis. This was denied. The father's case was that his children should know of his love for them, but as he had not seen them for three years the trial judge said that access would cause problems and disturbance: 'They may get to know their father but they may be disturbed by this. They may start to ask questions about his life, and they may wish to stay with him' (Bradley, 1987: 175). The Court of Appeal agreed while taking the view that the father's homosexuality was not the crucial factor in denying access but only the last in a series. It was the 'additional problem of the reaction of the children when they got to know that their father had sexual activities or a sexual life, which does not conform to the statistical norm' (Bradley, 1987: 176).

Male homosexuality was presented as a major problem in *Morris* v. *Morris* (1983) where photographs described as having 'a strong homosexual content', which involved the future stepfather, were found by the child's father. Both parents wanted custody, but the child – a twelve-year-old boy – wanted to live with his mother. There were practical problems in the father's household but notwithstanding these the 'risk situation' to a pubescent boy of the mother's household was considered too great. The Court of Appeal agreed. However, where a father had cared for his son for most of his life and there was 'no evidence that he had associations with other men which had any sort of impact on his home life' (*Walker* v. *Walker*, 1980 quoted in Bradley, 1987: 177) the risk was discounted by the Court of Appeal.

Lesbianism

Law has not criminalised lesbian sexual activity as such; nor has the lesbian emerged as a stigmatised identity in a manner similar to the male homosexual. But lesbian mothers applying to live with, or to have regular contact with, their children are difficult for family law judges to come to terms with. A possible reason for this is that there is a perceived dissonance between 'mother' and all that the word implies, and 'lesbian' which carries a different set of resonances. Faced with this problem of dissonance, courts resort to the external environment and general social attitudes.

> It will be difficult to imagine that this young boy could go through his adolescent period of development without feeling shame and embarrassment at having a mother who has elected to engage in sexual practices which are statistically abnormal. (Psychiatrist's report, cited by Crane, 1982: 122)

So, although the mother may be seen by the court as better qualified for child care than the father by reason of past experience or a 'natural bond', her femininity, which is affirmed by such a perception, is opened to question by her sexual preferences. The outcome of this dissonance is that instead of being preferred to the father where both offer equal advantages, the lesbian mother is seen as a threat to her children's welfare. In *W* v. *W* (1976) the Court of Appeal gave custody of her two daughters to the mother only because the father could not offer a suitable home. Whether the mother's lesbian relationship or her personality was at issue is not clear, but the Court of Appeal refrained from imposing a condition requested by the father, that the children should not be brought into contact with the mother's lesbian friends. Ormrod LJ said he understood the father's concern, but he left it:

> to the good sense of the mother to conduct her own personal life in such a way that it does not impinge too much on her children because I cannot really believe that she wants her twins to grow up as homosexual girls rather than as normal girls, but maybe I am wrong. (Bradley, 1987: 182)

The welfare of a child is better served by living with a parent with a stigmatised identity than in the care of a local authority of the state, as proposed by the father in *Re P* (1983). But a child going to live with a lesbian mother 'can only be countenanced by the courts when ... there is ... no other acceptable alternative form of custody' (*Re P*, 1983: 405). And 'for the future the progress of this child in this home must be regularly, carefully and discreetly watched by one of those trained to do so ...' (*Re P*, 1983: 406). This mother was described as a 'sensitive, articulate, and understanding woman', 'not one of those homosexuals who ... flaunt their homosexuality', 'discreet in her behaviour' (*Re P*, 1983: 403). The father's case for putting the child in the hands of the state and out of 'a secure and a warm environment' (1983: 404) was based on corruption and reputation. Corruption relates to good and bad example. Reputation relates 'expressions of ridicule and scorn' by some sections of the community and at a lesbian household, leading to teasing and embarrassment of the child (1983: 404). The Court of Appeal rejected the corruption argument but acknowledged the reputation argument.

Concern that children will be 'led into sexually deviant ways' seems to have been crucial to the denial of custody to the mother in *Eveson* v. *Eveson* (1980) and in *Re A* (1980). In *S* v. *S* (1980) a psychiatrist gave evidence that there was no such danger, but another psychiatrist referred to social embarrassment and hurt to the children if their mother's lesbian relationship became known. This factor, and the danger of exposure 'to ways of life of this kind' decided the trial judge in favour of the father. The Court of Appeal refused to interfere, despite a welfare report in favour of the mother. It seems that the 'reputation' argument carries weight with the courts. Whether this argument can stand up to close examination is doubtful, unless children are to be denied all contact with parents whose sexual preferences are for their own sex. This point is based on the idea that reputation is not confined to gossip about the parent with whom a child lives. It extends to parents as such, although living in an 'unusual' household may be more evident to friends. There is a difficulty here. What the courts appear to be saying is that secrecy about parental living arrangements will spare a child social embarrassment. No consideration of the burden of secrecy for a child is evident, except in the trial judgment in *C* v. *C* (1991). In that case the judge took the view that, as the child was bound to visit her mother, she would know of her lesbian relationship. If she lived in the father's household where lesbianism was viewed unfavourably this would cause difficulties. This practical reasoning did not find favour in the Court of Appeal.

In *M* v. *M* (1977) and *C* v. *C* (1991) the Court of Appeal took a normative approach to custody disputes between lesbian mothers and heterosexual fathers. This was justified 'because society is oriented and organised on the basis of heterosexual family relationships in spite of greater tendencies to toleration' (*M* v. *M*, 1977 quoted in Bradley, 1987: 184). Biology and the future of the human race were also used in support, and the norm of 'male parent figure and female parent figure'. Starting from the ideal environment for the upbringing of a child as 'the home of loving, caring and sensible parents' (*C* v. *C*, 1991: 225), and 'that the moral standards which are generally accepted in the society in which the child lives are more likely than not to promote his or her welfare' (1991: 227) the Court of Appeal said that the trial judge was wrong not to give significant weight to the mother's lesbian relationship as a negative factor. Despite this, on remission of the case for re-hearing, the Family Division of the High Court awarded custody to the mother, with whom the child had a strong bond.

Empirical evidence on the raising of children in lesbian households does not bear out the fears expressed by the judiciary. Examining three arguments against awarding custody to lesbian mothers, Tasker and Golombok (1991) review the available information. The first argument is that children with lesbian mothers are more likely to experience emotional and behavioral problems. The evidence reviewed suggests that children of lone, heterosexual mothers have more significant problems. The second argument is based on the belief that the gender identity and masculinity/femininity of children will be affected by being raised by a lesbian mother. Notions of example and role model are important here, as are the stigmatising of the 'abnormal'. The outcome of the review is that no firm conclusions can be drawn about gender identity or sexual preferences. The third argument is that based on external prejudice, teasing, embarrassment. Again there is no significant empirical evidence to support this. Although Tasker and Golombok admit that the studies reported have limitations, they also suggest that a mother's openness with her children makes it easier for them to handle any problems that arise. Their conclusion is that the courts should focus on good parenting practices, such as openness, sharing and understanding, rather than on sexuality. It is worth noting that a psychiatrist's evidence that the dangers to a child of living in a lesbian household tend to be overestimated resulted in an award of custody to the mother in *B* v. *B* (1991).

Research on children brought up by lesbian mothers, or by homosexual fathers, does not confirm commonly expressed fears about their future psychological, social or sexual orientations (Steel, 1990). Nevertheless, studies show how deeply embedded are these fears. A study of 29 lesbian mothers in custody disputes reports that 18 chose to settle, often against their own wishes as to outcome, and that of the remaining 11 only four received custody (Rights of Women, 1984).

Transsexuals and Transvestites
Cases on access to or custody of children of transsexuals do not feature in law reports. As post-operative transsexuals are dependent on surgical intervention it may be that approval for the operation is denied to persons who are parents of minor children. In cases of transvestism conditions about the maintenance of appropriate clothing and gender identity during visits by children have been imposed by the courts. This is done to avoid confusion for children who live in a world of gender divisions. Because women can, and often do, wear trousers, jackets, suits,

shirts, ties – all clothes considered appropriate for men, prohibitions on cross-dressing are usually applied only to men. The maintenance of masculinity, of boundaries around being male, seems to require greater social definition than the maintenance of femininity.

Conclusion

This chapter has explored how gender is engendered by one form of power in social life, by family law and its discourse. It has not been possible to address all aspects of family law, such as policies on the adoption or fostering of children where social workers make judgements about prospective parents on the basis of models of 'normality'. Problems that occur when an unorthodox household breaks up, and the law's attempts to impose a biological solution, have also been omitted (see Polikoff, 1990). What we have seen is the construction of women and men as binary opposites, with attributes of femininity and masculinity ascribed to them. Western philosophy since the Enlightenment has taken as its self-conception a version of itself as a 'rational' society. Reason is opposed to emotion, culture is opposed to nature, objectivity is opposed to subjectivity, self-control is opposed to feelings. The former are taken to be the exclusive property of men; the latter belong to women. In the broader culture masculinity as power is invisible, for, as Seidler says, 'the rule of men is simply taken as an expression of reason and "normality"' (Seidler, 1989: 4). Women and men are the losers by this as the former are subordinated and the latter are estranged from themselves, 'as they learn to think of themselves in terms of the neutral standards of reason'.

The purpose of this chapter is to make space for the voices of others – voices that in the past were silenced in the name of reason – to speak. A legal forum may not be the place to hear of such voices, if rationality, law and masculinity are associated and connected (Collier, 1991a). But, as we have seen, family law does not draw on a privileged, technical discourse but on 'common sense', the 'reasonable man', 'public policy'. Law is a way of knowing, of defining the 'normal', of stigmatising the 'unusual', of silencing that which is 'known' as irrational, unscientific, odd, extraordinary. It is not just that experience gets translated into legal terms or ignored, as some writers claim. It is not just that powerful men can impose their representations of male experience of power on all in the name of universal law as reason. The claims of law are stronger than that, are coercive, and 'legal interpretation takes place in a field of pain and death' (Cover, 1986: 1601). There is a violence in the claim to know, to prescribe the normal, to rule out ways of being; there is individual hurt and pain, the opening up of others' experiences to ridicule, shame and hatred. Grbich (1991) argues that law is the embodied imaginings of certain powerful men. It is not the projection of the experience of all its subjects. But as Seidler (1989) reminds us, it does violence to many men as they attempt self-domination and a denial of emotion, feelings and desire in the name of masculinity.

We must not forget that whatever the pain in constructing and reconstructing a masculine identity it brings with it the values of heterosexual male superiority. Being opposite to women, having the attributes of reason, is to be superior to women. Male sexual identity is about defending masculine attributes, about shaping oneself:

> for they are reassuring mirrors that reflect back an idealised image of masculinity and a sense of belonging. Our sexual identities are a lifelong project. We can attempt to carry through the ideology of male superiority with is consequences, and try to emulate the archetypal image that embodies the idealised man of our particular class and culture. (Rutherford, 1988: 24)

Because the power to define, to give meaning, resides with orthodox, heterosexual men from a particular class, they arrogate to themselves the 'normal'. They do not see themselves as gendered beings – that is for women and for stigmatised men. Power hides its own mechanisms. It is for other men to make us see masculinities, and to bring these into question.

Reason is identified with the calculation of self-interest, and with control of self and one's environment. In traditional masculinist terms this means avoiding dependence, and the acknowledgement of emotions and needs. This leads to a conception of self which is projected as an ideal, universal conception of human nature. The binary system woman/man bifurcates this version of human nature with the projection on to women of qualities of emotionality and irrationality, qualities shared by human beings in the idea of feelings. The detailed analysis of the gendered language used in child-custody cases is designed to illustrate this. It is not being suggested here that masculinity is fixed in an inescapable category. The plural form, masculinities, has been used where possible (Segal, 1990). Nor is it being suggested that femininity and woman are fixed, stable, ontological categories. If women appear to be better at nurturing children, if nurturance and femininity seem to go together, this is for historical and social reasons.

Feminist theories, and the work of cultural feminists in particular, do project another conception of human nature. Based on identification with others, stemming from an awareness of subordination, these theories valorise feelings, and an integrated self. What is involved is a challenge to cultural conceptions of the rational self, separate from others, controlled. These theories talk of empathy, of morality based on intimate relationships, of false polarities of the rational/the emotional of rational morality (see Chodorow, 1978; Gilligan, 1982; West, 1988). Chapter 6 discusses this further in terms of the individual 'seen' by family law and conceptions of human nature.

6
The Child as Legal Object

How do children fit into a legal framework? Is it accurate to represent children as having a juridical existence in any real sense? I want to suggest that the child 'seen' by family law is an object and not a legal subject. To sum up, at the beginning, children's subjectivity is denied by legal discourse, with some exceptions. By this I mean that children's ability to act as juridical subjects is non-existent in law. There is a space in legal discourse, an emptiness, where a child's individuality should be. General social conditions of children's vulnerability and dependence largely account for this, but also, perhaps, adult power. There are reasons of legal method also. Consider, for example, the standard legal subject that legal discourse constructs for itself. This subject is rational and reasonable, qualities that law does not attribute to children. Legal officials dealing with children may do so with empathy, but this does not overcome the legal difficulties of the incapable subject.

There are a number of levels at which law's denial of children's subjectivity operates. First there is the obvious legal point that the full legal subject is taken to be a person over the age of 18 – an emancipated person. Despite the development of the concept of the 'mature minor' (*Gillick* v. *West Norfolk and Wisbech Area Health Authority*, 1986) the child is not emancipated, in the old sense of Roman law. Second, there is the point that the child lacks attributes necessary to the legal subject. It is not just a lack of age, but an ascribed lack of autonomy, self-control, common sense, independence. Political theorists of the past, such as Hobbes (1966: 191), Locke (1967: 47) and Rousseau (1968, 1: 50) have denied the capacity of female children ever to develop these attributes in a full sense; male children are said to acquire them at 18, which is the age of emancipation. Third, when the family legal process does consider children, it usually does so through a paternalistic discourse. Whether the talk is of 'needs', 'welfare', or 'best interests' of the child, it is adults who interpret this. Analysis of this process reveals that the focus of the law is inevitably drawn to competing adults; this is so whether they are seeking possession of the child as object, or are engaged in disciplinary power struggles over the child.

What type of 'individual' is constructed by law as legal subject? Some writers argue that law constructs for itself a person based on the white middle-class heterosexual male (Naffine, 1990). Although this person is an artefact who does not correspond to particular persons, nevertheless he is said to have certain qualities closer to a stereotypical male than to others. The characteristics in question are those of an atomised individual: separateness, autonomy, rationality, calculation. We must bear in mind, however, that a variety of legal artefacts are created, depending on the branch of law in question. Thus, economic man is different from family man. Allen (1987) says that:

> legal discourse constructs for itself a standard human subject, endowed with consciousness, reason, foresight, intentionality, an awareness of right and wrong and a knowledge of the law of the land. (1987: 23)

It may be, however, that this description is best confined to the criminal law. It is more likely that law constructs for itself a variety of individuals, and that its stance on its subject is contingent. This leads to a certain incoherence and contradiction when the artefacts clash.

Family law discourse, as we have seen in Chapter 5, constructs persons over the age of 18 as gendered in opposition to one another. Smart (1989b: 1) argues that the family law is a vehicle for the allocation of children between women and men, and that children form part of the nexus of power within family relations. The definition of power involved here is as 'an inevitable aspect of all social relations' (1989b: 2). Parents have power over children, but children also provide a site for power struggles between adults:

> the presence of children in a household creates the potential of a power nexus that parents can exploit positively or negatively in relation to one another ... and the subsequent power claims that parenthood potentiates are linked to the question of gender. (1989b: 3)

This chapter argues that because children are not legal subjects, because children constitute an arena for parental power struggles or power exercise – or a site of operation of various professional groups, such as social workers, doctors, the police, the 'psy' disciplines – because children do not have legal rights on a par with other rights holders as understood in liberal discourse, consequently there is a space, an emptiness, which enables the conversion of children into legal objects. The very language of writers who refer to children as a 'site', indicates this. Given the nature of legal method and law's discourse it may be impossible for children not to be objects. Or, as already suggested, adult power may preclude juridical status for children:

> The discourse of judges and lawyers who claim to take into account only the interest of the child (as opposed to the interests of each of the parents) should be countered by showing that, when they speak of the child, they are always and inevitably speaking of something else – the father, the mother, the family itself. (Thèry, 1989: 83)

The Language of Knowing Subject and Known Object

Theorists of late modernity are agreed in condemning the Cartesian legacy of dichotomies in Enlightenment thought, where rationality is opposed to irrationality, culture to nature, masculinity to femininity. In that tradition only the rational, knowing subject who knows the object can arrive at truth through abstract, universalistic thought. As an alternative these theorists posit plurality of knowledge, of truths, of ways of seeing. Knowledge, subjects and objects are said to be constituted in discourse; metanarratives are rejected (Rorty, 1979). This has lead to an attack on the subject and to the decentring of man as knowing subject (Heidegger, 1977). The idea of a single subject, of a dominant identity, is under attack. What is happening in the late twentieth century has been called the fragmentation of identity. This leads to an anti-essentialist position which challenges the way the subject has been constituted in western texts. Foucault says that there are no essential objects or subjects, only individuals caught in a network of historic power relations; and that discourse about knowledge creates subjects and deploys power. The idea is to question claims to know, particularly where the claim is about others. Subjects for Foucault are concrete historical and cultural beings constituted by discourse. The discourses in question are those that created the subjectivity of individuals in the first place (Foucault, 1980). These insights have given birth to new ways of talking theory. It is more doubtful whether new ways of talking law can follow.

Family law ways of talking about children are paternalistic and predictive: the child's welfare is central to decisions, whether about upbringing, adoption, residence. Behind the word 'welfare' lies a claim to knowledge of what is in the child's interests. In giving a decision about a child's future a court has to couch its justification in the language of welfare; this is a claim to know and to predict (Children Act 1989, s. 1 (1)). Those adults in conflict over the child's future put forward their positions as in the child's best interests, as do the 'psy' experts called in to advise or give evidence. That there is doubt over knowledge and prediction then becomes obvious. But because the structure of the law requires this method of proceeding, these doubts have to be quelled.

Children as Objects

It is not just that children are objects of knowledge, nor only that adults claim to know better what is best for the child. Children, metaphysical or real, are objects of desire, for those who want to be parents. In the recent past law has been called upon to define issues of parentage of children born as a result of commission, sale or donation of genetic material, and womb-leasing. Since 1926 legal adoption has been possible in England and Wales. In the legal and social talk and texts which operate in this area it is evident that a child is a valuable commodity. There is resistance to the idea of sale, which is illegal in relation to adoption (Adoption Act 1976, s. 57). Surrogacy contracts are unenforceable (Human Fertilization and Embryology Act 1990). Yet the parenthood wish makes children desirable objects, and capitalist society normally values things on the market. The ideology that places children beyond the market calls on another tradition, that of human rights. This tradition of fundamental human rights derives from deontological philosophy, that is, from a tradition which sees the person as valuable, possessed of inalienable rights. The question becomes one of whether these rights are acquired only at the age of majority, or whether it is the exercise of rights which is delayed. Later in this chapter we shall discuss whether this tradition has meaning in relation to children.

The placing of children beyond the market opens the way for those agents endowed by law with the power of 'placement' of children. There are three points to be made here. First, the producers of children, namely women, are denied the power to dispose of their products. As Okin (1990, Ch. 4) points out, this contradicts the general libertarian view that persons own themselves and the fruits of their labour. For example, Robert Nozick accepts that 'a free system' will allow a person 'to sell himself into slavery' (1974: 331). It is not that Okin advocates the sale of children by mothers, her object is to draw attention to the neglect of family and gender in theories of justice. My point here is to identify the arguments that place children beyond the market, and to note how this creates a zone of operation for those with power to dispose of children – not for money.

The second point is that, outside the market children become priceless. This point is not confined to the banning of children from the market, but it extends to the instatement of children as household gods in child-centred families. This means that those professionals endowed with medical skills or administrative powers, and who decide who shall receive infertility treatment or clearance to adopt, are able to act as brokers.

Finally, the pricelessness of children is worthy of contemplation. Our children are priceless in a variety of ways: they are unique; they are family icons that are the centre of the nuclear unit; they are beyond price; they are beyond the market. The theory that places children beyond the market calls on a humanistic tradition, on the modern repudiation of slavery and on our instinctive repudiation of a trade in children. We can contrast this with proposals from the law and economics school for a market in babies designed to increase the efficiency of the family. Elizabeth Landes and Richard Posner (1978) observe that the demand for children is far greater than the supply. Government agencies, such as local authorities in Britain, have a virtual monopoly over the supply of adoptees, and regulate the conditions under which children can be imported from abroad. Landes and Posner argue that a free market in the sale of babies would have the following advantages: it would release many children from foster care and children's homes, whose biological parents at present have no incentive to make them available for adoption; the cost to the state of placing children would be passed to adoptive parents and baby producers; and the market would be a more efficient instrument in finding homes for children as the price mechanism serves to protect the valuable object.

Many commentators object to the commodification of children inherent in this proposal. Bennett (1991: 214) says that a premium would be paid for the perfect child, stigmatising children with disabilities or regarded as the 'wrong' race or colour. Children might be able to sue the birth mother because of a lower market value due to disability caused by the mother's negligence, resulting in purchase by a poor family. Purchasers might sue for breach of warranty, if the child did not match up to contract specification. Prichard (1984: 349) pictures a market in second-hand children deemed unsatisfactory, as purchasers 'trade-up' by buying new-borns. To counter the language of economic rationality an appeal to humanistic values has to be deployed. This tells us something about our attitudes and feelings, but it does not justify the delay of children's juridical status.

The objectification of children inherent in proposals for a baby market is evident. The question is whether the existing legal discourse, grounded in humanism, succeeds in avoiding objectification. In order to answer this question we shall consider disputes between persons with parental powers, issues concerning who bears the costs of child rearing, and debates about intervention by the 'child saving professions'.

Parental Disputes

Where parents do not agree on the upbringing of a child, or on the child's residence, or on the administration of the child's property, the Children Act 1989 lays down the general principle that the child's welfare is paramount in deciding such questions (s. 1). Ultimately it is for a court to obtain the knowledge necessary for this prediction. However, doubt as to courts' past record in this regard creeps in with section 1 (5) of the Act which states that 'the court should not make an order unless to do so is considered better for the child than making no order'. The Law Commission (1988, no 170) has taken the view that court orders, particularly those concerning residence and contact of children of divorcing parents, have the effect of escalating parental conflict and alienating the child from one parent. There is research evidence that the children who fare best when parents part are those who maintain a positive relationship with both (see Wallerstein and Kelly, 1980; Wallerstein and Blakeslee, 1986). Behind this lies the view that law should intervene as little as possible, leaving parents to 'know best' and settle their children's future privately. This is an example of law's retreat from a claim to knowledge of children's best interests, an unsustainable claim, for law. But to what extent does it recognise children's subjectivity? And to what extent does law claim to know the child's best interests in other circumstances?

The relationship between parents and child has been restructured in terms of parental responsibility (Children Act 1989, s. 3). According to this legal construction childhood is a preparation for adulthood, and parents are responsible 'for caring for and raising the child to be a properly developed adult both physically and morally' (Lord Mackay, 1988, *Hansard*, HL, vol 502, col 490). Until then the child is in a legal limbo, lacking autonomy, legally dependent on those with parental responsibility. However, the child's wishes can be considered in court proceedings. This is a limited recognition of the child as subject.

Where family proceedings come before a court and a question arises about the welfare of a child, then the court can make orders concerning the child's future residence and contacts, or ordering or prohibiting the exercise of certain aspects of parental responsibility (Children Act 1989, s. 8), provided the child is under 16, or in exceptional cases between 16 and 18 (s. 9 (6)). The welfare principle governs the making of such orders and the court is directed to a checklist of seven relevant factors in determining welfare. The first of these is 'the ascertainable wishes and feelings of the child concerned (considered in the light of his age and understanding) (s. 1 (3) (a)). As welfare is a consideration in the making of an order placing a child in the care of the local authority (s. 31) the child's wishes are relevant. In addition, the court must consider the arrangements for contact with family members or other significant persons in the child's life, and invite the parties to the proceedings to comment on the proposed arrangements (s. 34 (11)). Again, welfare is relevant. In adoption there is also a requirement that the court has regard to the child's wishes (Adoption Act 1976, s. 6). However, welfare is a double-edged sword, and may provide a reason for ignoring what the child says. It is 'doubtful whether the court would follow the child's views if it thought that to do so would be prejudicial to his welfare ... the probability is that the court could simply dispose of the case by holding that the child was not mature enough to make the decision in question' (White et al., 1990: 1.11).

In general the person under 18 is a child. However, the doctrine of the 'mature minor' enunciated in the Gillick case (1986) leaves scope for the assertion of autonomy. In addition, certain legal provisions use 16 as the age of self-determination (Education Act 1944; Children Act 1989, s. 9 (6); Family Law Reform Act 1969). Notwithstanding this legal deference to development as a continual process, it is for adults with parental responsibility initially, and ultimately for the courts, to determine the child's welfare; this decision does not belong to the child. Some indication that the courts will listen to the child's point of view can be discerned in recent cases in which children are said to 'divorce' their parents. Under the Children Act 1989, section 8, the courts have power to make residence orders settling the arrangements as to the person with whom a child is to live. Children may make an application, if the court is satisfied that the child has sufficient understanding (s. 10 (8)). The courts also have power to make a prohibited steps order, and children have used this where a parent has attempted to force a change of residence.

Children Come First?

Children may be objects of desire to some would-be parents but the cost of raising a child has become a matter of political debate as to where it should fall. In the government White Paper *Children Come First* (1990, Cmnd 1264), which preceded the Child Support Act 1991, children are seen in terms of a 'maintenance bill'. Although the discussion is of 'the benefit of a child', the focus is on ensuring 'that parents honour their legal and moral responsibility to maintain their own children whenever they can afford to do so' (1990: 2.1). The needs of children are stated to be primarily defined by parents and to depend on their financial means. The needs of a new partner are not to take priority over a child because this 'is not putting the interests of the children first' (3.16). The language of 'rights' is avoided, being replaced instead by terms such as: 'it is nevertheless right that a child should look first to his own natural parents for his maintenance' (3.19); 'personal responsibility towards children is too important a principle to be ignored' (3.30); 'it is not right that the absent parent should choose to transfer his obligation to pay maintenance to the state if he can afford to meet that obligation himself' (5.33). The 'rights of children' are only mentioned in the context of opposition to the wishes of the caring parent who declines to claim maintenance because she wishes to avoid contact with the absent parent (5.31). There is no discussion of the wishes of children or of how they might enforce their rights of maintenance against parents. The object is to create an administrative agency for the collection of child support as has been done by the Child Support Act 1991.

The purpose of underlining the official language of child support is to convey to the reader the artificiality of attempts to identify the legal subjectivity of a child, whether in terms of rights or autonomy. The language of rights in this context structures an opposition between children and parents. But children are unable to claim the right to parental support personally, should they wish to do so.

The Child Savers

Jasmine Beckford (1985), Heidi Koseda (1986), Tyra Henry (1987), Kimberley Carlile (1987), Doreen Aston (1989), these are some of the names of children whose deaths at the hands of adult parental figures have resulted in legal inquiries and reports. The search for social work practices, police procedures and legal safeguards to protect children produces inquiries and legislative reforms, most recently the Children Act 1989. This section refers to one such inquiry, that by Lord Justice Butler-Sloss, *Child Abuse in Cleveland* (1988, Cmnd 412).

What the report reveals is not only that children's lack of legal subjectivity is a problem on a practical level, but also that it creates a space in which professional single mindedness, and sometimes rivalries, can flourish. The reader may think that the phrase 'lack of legal subjectivity' is merely a code for the obvious difficulties of communicating with children because of their age and inexperience. But the phrase is used to draw attention to the powerlessness of children and to the scepticism with which adults listen to their accounts of their activities or experiences. The giving of evidence in criminal trials in court provides an example (Spencer and Flin, 1990). The assumption that a child is not competent to give evidence has been removed by the Criminal Justice Act 1991, which makes video recordings of a child's statement admissible as evidence in chief. Nevertheless, the recording will only be admissible if the child is available for cross-examination at the trial, which requirement reveals a distrust of children's stories, but also leaves the child witness open to intimidation in court. The rules of evidence remain paramount, perhaps because of concern for the presumption of innocence of the accused. One of the principal objectives of the Report of the Home Office Advisory Group on Video Evidence (1989: 2.26) was that 'children who come within the ambit of our proposals ought never to be required to appear in public as witnesses in the Crown Court, whether in open court or protected by screens or closed circuit television unless they wish to do so'. This has not been achieved and children may be cross-examined at the trial, possibly after a considerable lapse of time. We need to think further about what justice requires here. At present safeguarding the rights of the accused is the paramount concern; on the other hand adverse consequences for individual children may follow from cross-examination, children may break down and be unable to continue their evidence in court, and the idea that children's voices cannot be trusted may be reinforced.

The Cleveland Report (1988) reveals a lack of co-operation between the professional groups, doctors, nurses, police, social workers, and lawyers who were involved with the allegations of sex abuse, and with the taking into care of children. This is not just a question of a failure of communication, but also of professional systems which do not interconnect. Each group remained mired in its own professional language and practices, in its own definitions and paradigms, in its own ways of seeing. Although all those involved referred to the 'welfare' of the children, there was no apparent agreement on how this was to be interpreted. Carty and Mair (1990: 397) identify the welfare principle as follows:

> There are standards which are appealed to *as if objective*, but which have, in fact, no referent. These legal signs mediate a 'reality' which does not have positive consistency because it is objectification of a void, of a discontinuity opened up in reality by the presence of the signifier itself.

But it is also the legal denial of the child's subjectivity that requires the construction of the paternalistic notion of welfare and the consequent void occupied by the knowledges and powers of the various professions.

The Cleveland tale, as told in the report (1988, Cmnd 412), is of scientific claims of identification of child abuse by paediatricians at levels higher than previously. What followed was a crisis in which conflict between different professional 'truths' and procedures was evident: 'There was a rising conflict between agencies attempting to grapple with a serious and delicate problem without an agreed systematic approach' (1988, Cmnd 412: 61). This meant that parents and foster parents could be told very little. On the one hand, medical diagnosis on the basis of an 'anal dilation' test was claimed as scientific by its users; on the other hand, police surgeons and a variety of 'experts' voiced doubts. A common point of reference was lacking, despite child-saving ambitions. As the numbers of children detected as abused rose, and the children were taken into care by social workers, the police lagged behind because their procedures required additional evidence. Eventually they 'retreated from the multi-disciplinary approach into an entrenched position' (1988, Cmnd 412: 244).

For proponents of the theory of autopoietic systems, as discussed in Chapter 2, the Cleveland tale provides some empirical confirmation. The paediatricians developed anal dilation as a means of detection of child abuse which satisfied them and which they regarded as scientific. Within their subsystem such proof was a verification of diagnosis. Their belief in the truth of their findings appears to have been genuine. But their subsystem barely overlapped with that of the police, who needed 'to look for substantial corroboration' (1988, Cmnd 412: 65), and to satisfy the evidential requirements for criminal prosecution. Further-more, the police objected to the taking of photographs of the alleged victims, which they believed to be unnecessary (1988, Cmnd 412: 94). Social workers were concerned to work with the children for purposes of therapy and to obtain disclosure of what had occurred. They therefore used the legal procedures at their disposal to remove the children from their homes. Working within their ideological formation they followed the dictates of their training.

A revealing subplot in the drama was played by members of the nursing profession. Concern with the daily care of the sick is the first priority for nurses in hospitals. Not only were they perturbed that children who were admitted to hospital for reasons unrelated to sex abuse were subjected to the anal dilation test and diagnosed as abused, but the confinement of other children to the hospital resulted in a certain chaotic running about. Not surprisingly this upset the daily routine and the order of priorities. Some of these children were siblings of those first detected, later brought in for examination. Nurses also complained of children being awoken from sleep to provide a control for comparison with children identified as abused. To sum up, they were unhappy about the way the detection progressed.

Carty and Mair (1990) argue that each agency charged with the care of children sees the child as within its own domain:

> They search according to their own rules – they hunt for their own signs – they seek to apply their own sanctions. 'Experts differed in the weight they placed on particular signs' (Report: 189). They apparently share the same aim – the abused child – but their searches are directed towards diverse and distinct aspects. The police seek evidence, the doctors seek a physical sign, the social workers seek disclosure. (1990: 406)

The authors emphasise that, even if the agencies are credited with concern for children, they do not necessarily have the same impetus. In particular they suggest that the paediatricians and social workers 'were to some extent driven on by a search for knowledge, displaying in their quest the need for confirmation of their theory rather than an unbiased inquiry for the "truth"' (1990: 408). But their most compelling criticism is that amid these various truths the child was forgotten. Whether this was because children's stories were discredited, or because children's voices cannot be heard, is not clear. We need to ask ourselves what procedures exist in the practices of those professions dealing with children to enable children to speak and to be heard. But if adults cannot hear because the subsystem to which they belong, and which practices its discipline on children, is closed to the child's voice, then my concern with empowering the child is vital.

The subjectivity of a child is not necessarily comparable to that of the adult the child becomes, let alone to that of an objectified standard made by legislators. Photographs of ourselves as children are photographs of strangers, except that the strangers are our previous selves. Yet Susie, aged three, was able to tell the tale of being sexually abused and thrown into a cesspit in such a way as to lead to the conviction of her tormentor (Jones, 1987: 677).

In the name of searching for the abused child, the individual child rarely appears. The experts examine parts of the child, the inquiry concentrates on adult representations of the child – 'the voices of the children (are) not heard'. (Carty and Mair: 407, citing Report, 1988: 45).

Rights as Answers?

Is the answer to the problem of children's lack of legal subjectivity, of the legal treatment of children as objects, to enter into a rights discourse? The construction of children as rights holders has been undertaken in law at a variety of levels, from the most general in the International Declaration of the Rights of the Child, through the European Convention on Human Rights, to domestic law. These statements about children have a significance as symbols and rhetoric, and it is important that they should be made. But does this rights talk overcome the lack of legal subjectivity discussed earlier? Does law allow children to assert those fundamental human rights contained in, for example, the Convention on the Rights of the Child, adopted by the United Nations General Assembly on 20 November 1989?

The paradox contained in this chapter is that even when children are constructed as rights holders it is difficult for them to assert their rights. The reasons are practical, political and legal. Young children are completely and unavoidably dependent on those who have power over their lives. Childhood is a stage in the life-cycle, and the forms of disability children suffer from are peculiar to nonage. In practical terms, one cure for an individual child's powerlessness comes with reaching the age recognised by law for liberty or autonomy. Further judicial development of the idea of the 'mature minor' – of autonomy as a gradual process – rather than arrival at one fell swoop at the age of 18 is a possible step towards the realisation of subjectivity at an earlier stage. Articles 12–15 of the Convention on the Rights of the Child appear to recognise a form of subjectivity, as they relate to freedom of opinion, freedom of expression, freedom of thought, conscience and religion, and freedom of association. However, this has been strongly criticised as contradictory with the child's lack of juridical capacity to exercise these rights (Thèry, 1992; Mallet and Monier, 1992).

Political constructions of rights, perhaps later embodied in positive law, often emanate in a claim by a dispossessed group. Such claims may be based on denial of a pre-existing or fundamental right for which recognition is demanded. In other words, the claim is based on conceptions of equality or liberty, and often is for parity with other members of the community. Whether the right that is claimed derives from some absolutist ideal based on natural law, or from humanistic notions about respect for others, the appeal is ethical. Whether the appeal is for the community to live up to the standards it has set itself, or to extend its existing notions of rights, it is couched in terms of something that is already there – an idea, a language, a principle. It is this which enables the making of the claim, and its ultimate recognition.

I want to suggest that it is difficult to bring children into the framework of rights for three reasons associated with practical politics. First there are the practical reasons mentioned above, to do with children's unavoidable dependence. Secondly rights talk grew out of a repudiation of paternalism, and often involves an appeal over the heads of those in power, urging the powerless to claim their rights. Paternalistic language is still considered an appropriate way of talking about children because of their vulnerability, and the powers in their lives are concentrated not just in particular places or buildings, but are also in the home. Thirdly manifesto rights such as those contained in the Convention of the Rights of the Child cannot be claimed unless and until practices are established that determine against whom claims on behalf of a particular child may be lodged (O'Neill, 1988). What is required is legislation, but the state is cautious, and adult agents are still needed to act for the child. As Onora O'Neill says (1988: 462): 'Those who urge respect for children's rights must address not children but those whose action may affect children.'

The legal reasons why constructing children as rights holders may not work is that rights untranslated into positive law do not tell us what should be done. Where children's rights are placed on the political agenda this usually results in the creation of social practices and institutions rather than in the direct construction of a right with a corresponding duty on some adult, which is enforceable in court. Again the practical problems of children's unavoidable lack of capacity are raised. Of course, parents and others in a relationship with a child, such as teachers, doctors, officers of state institutions for children, have positive duties to that child. But these are based on the assumption of care which has been undertaken. The specific content of these duties depends on legislation, but also on institutional practices.

Rights talk in a political context is often adversarial. Different conceptions of what makes lives worthwhile and of fairness across lives conflict. As Steven Lukes sees it: 'The notion of "rights" neatly expresses this double concern: we claim as our "rights" what will fairly protect our interests. So it is no surprise that the natural way to express political conflicts is often as a clash between rights to various liberties ...' (1990: 64). It is not only the adversarial nature of rights that may make the notion unadoptable by children, but also the claim to liberty involved. Children are not free, in the sense that adults are free. Children are under a regime, that of parental, educational and state control, and family law reflects this. Where a court is satisfied that a child 'is suffering, or likely to suffer significant harm', due to 'the child's being beyond parental control', then she or he may be placed in the care of, or under the supervision of, the local authority (Children Act 1989, s. 31 (1) (2)). What this means is that the state will attempt to act as substitute parent in controlling children if their welfare is interpreted as so demanding. If we conclude that notions of rights, useful though they may be in symbolic terms, do not adequately express 'the drama of being a child', where shall we turn?

Two possible alternative ways of expressing the relationship of children to their carers in legal terms can be suggested. These are the theory of fundamental obligations, and the legal concept of trust. Onora O'Neill (1988) argues that theories of fundamental obligations are better for children because of theoretical difficulties in relation to rights, in particular the incomplete, indirect and indeterminate nature of rights for children. In her view there is a lack of clarity about what should be received by the child. Furthermore, in political terms, useful though the concept of rights may be to powerless adults, it does not recognise how children are different. The rhetoric of rights merely serves to remind adults of their duties. O'Neill proposes the conceptualisation of the relationship between adults and children in terms of fundamental obligations which may be a more realistic form of expression. This is a constructivist account of the ethical base for legal claims by children. Its advantage is that it allows a wider base which can encompass what O'Neill designates imperfect obligations, such as the obligation of kindness to children, which cannot be universal and specific. Obligations can be identified successively, rather than requiring identification of all in order to identify any; in this sense they lack the 'all or nothing' quality of rights. But although O'Neill's project may provide a more comprehensive ethical base for children's legal claims than does the theory of fundamental rights, it does not entirely overcome the problem of violation of obligation and whether children have a remedy. In other words, it may provide a satisfactory theoretical and political account, but in legal terms there are a myriad of practical problems. Not the least of these remains the problem of children as legal actors in the making of claims, or the imposing of obligations.

If we approach the question of children and adults in terms of an expanded legal concept of trust certain interesting ideas follow. At present, where children own or inherit something they cannot deal with as legal owners, such as property, so the concept of the trust is used. Although children can be equitable owners or beneficiaries, the legal ownership is with the trustees, who must account for their stewardship. On reaching majority the beneficiaries may take action against the trustees for breach of trust if there has been mismanagement. The duties of trustees are clearly defined and stem from the idea of conscience; the standard of conduct required is high. What I want to suggest is that since we are willing to use such a notion for the care of the infant's property, consideration should be given to its extension to the care of the infant's person.

Legal acknowledgement of the violation of a trust by adults in a relationship of care with a child already exists. Criminal law protects physical integrity; family law has mechanisms for the removal of the child from home. Courts are beginning to allow civil suit by adults in connection with abuses suffered while children. For example, suit by a woman alleging mental illness and psychological disturbance as a result of being sexually abused as a child was allowed to proceed despite a delay of 12 years between the attainment of the age of majority and the issuing of a writ (*Stubbings* v. *Webb*, 1991). Suit for false imprisonment has been successfully brought by a woman against her father for marrying her off, at the age of 15 to the Yemeni son of a family friend without her knowledge. A secret ceremony took place in Birmingham, and the father then persuaded his daughter to travel from the United Kingdom to Yemen on the pretext of a holiday. The woman was detained against her will for eight years in a form of marriage (*Family Law*, 1991: 164).

That adults are beginning to demand a public account of what happened to them as children is clear. Those so seeking do not seem to be interested in compensation so much as in justice. They want, however retrospectively, a legal statement that what happened to them was wrong. This is a desire for an acknowledgement of a violation of trust by a parent figure. Furthermore, the Criminal Injuries Compensation Board has advertised the fact that compensation is available from public funds for victims of child abuse, whether the crime was committed by a parent figure or another person with access to the child. The extension of the board's powers to cover crimes in the family since 1979, a power which was previously omitted in the name of 'family privacy', is evidence of community condemnation of violation of trust, and that the wider community acknowledges responsibility for what happens to children. In the period April 1989 to March 1990 there were 4,825 claims by minors who were victims of abuse (1991, Cmnd 1365). It is true that retrospective community accountability in this context is for the harm caused to persons as children, but it implies a recognition of responsibility. The ideas of retrospective accountability and compensation, combined with responsibility for today's children, must include the idea of prevention of the harm in the first place. Bringing ideas of carer and community responsibility into the form of a trust concept, containing accountability of parents as trustees to the community, and suit for breach of trust, might have a hortatory effect on adult carers.

Two objections to such a proposal can be identified; the first is based on the legalisation of intimate relationships. A cartoon of an incredulous father sitting at the table, asking his child 'You say that if I make you drink your milk, you'll sue me?' sums up the objections to the growing legalisation of human relationships (Galanter, 1992: 13). But if the trust concept can bring together elements of disparate claims and adult vindications of childhood injustices the price of legalisation may be worth paying. A second objection is that if parental rights are really parental trusts this thinking leads to unacceptable curtailment of freedom: parents might have to be licensed before they could reproduce; pregnant women might be forced to undergo a battery of tests and controls for the sake of the priceless child; the spectre of state control, intrusive professionals, examination of all parents as if they were adopters, threatens liberty. Experiences of the activities of the state in this domain are not encouraging. Finding an equilibrium between community responsibility to future members, the trust that children and the community place in parents, and parental freedom is a difficult balancing act. And yet the idea of trust is attractive, if only because it expresses our cultural attitude to children as priceless.

Kymlicka (1991: 91) argues that the logic of parental trust leads to a demanding standard whereby probable harms to children are grounds for legal controls, such as regulation, licensing, or prohibition. Such controls are expressed by law in its regulation of human fertilisation and reproduction and in its refusal to enforce surrogacy contracts. In this sense children are priceless. Yet when it comes to actual parenting the law intervenes only when there is evidence of significant harm, or a likelihood thereof (Children Act 1989, s. 31 (1) (2)). The stand taken by the state is to value children as beyond the market, while recognising that parental freedom and the limits of law restrict activist intervention. As Kymlicka points out, this is an incoherent position as it attempts to combine state conceptions of the good with individual liberty and autonomy. Yet if children are considered as actors, rather than as objects of state or parental actions, then their freedom must be valued equally alongside that of parents.

It may be further objected that this chapter is written as if the world consisted only of children and families; in other words, factors of economic hardship, lack of support for abuse prevention programmes, the generational cycle of abuse, are omitted. It is not intended to suggest that legal changes in the way children are seen by law are sufficient to alter parental and professional behaviour. This is merely one of the necessary conditions for the recognition of developing autonomy in the state we call minority. But the denial of children's legal subjectivity, of their juridical capacity to act, is a problem in any theory of justice. My proposal concerning the enlargement of the concept of the trust to encompass the child's person, in addition to property, is made as a potentially new way of conceptualising the relationship of adult and child. This is particularly apposite if the problems of recognising children's juridical capacity remain insurmountable. The language of trust may overcome, in part at least, the problem of law's denial of children's subjectivity. I realise that this proposal is largely remedial, in that it does not overcome the paralysis induced by children's vulnerability and incompleteness. Children will be constructed as beneficiaries of a trust, and become subjects in that way. There is a hortatory element in such a restructuring of concepts.

7
Family Law as Conversation

How are we to approach family law as told to us in various texts, in cases, statutes, textbooks? How are we to discern the messages, the values, the subtexts, that are immanent or embedded in what we read? How can we identify the values assumed in various manifestations of law? What are the stories told to us of family conflicts and disputes that go to law, and become the stuff of which law is made? Do these stories represent what was told, or have they been transformed by lawyers, judges and others, by law's procedures and practices? And what of the stories untold in law because the silent cannot speak or lawyers cannot hear? To talk about these questions we must think about what family law was, is, and is about to be.

A central problem in family law today is a lack of an agreed basis for legislation and decision making. Although the judiciary may eschew moralising, other than to refer to certain ways of living as 'unusual', nevertheless certain family forms and choices are privileged by law. The themes of Chapters 3 and 5 have played on this point. Having come from an authoritarian, patriarchal and religious base, family law is faced with its tradition. This is a tradition that cannot accommodate the 'other', in the sense of the non-conformist, the stigmatised identity, the subordinated. As we saw in Chapter 6 children can be accommodated by family law only through turning them into legal objects.

The problem of a tradition that attempts to hear hitherto silent voices is not negligible. But what is the basis on which these voices can speak and be heard? What language is to be used to reach the family law makers? Is it possible to listen to those who speak from outside tradition? Alastair MacIntyre (1981: 227) identifies the lack of practical agreement on a conception of justice as a threat to society. He finds not only

> an inability to agree upon the relative importance of the virtue concepts and an even more fundamental inability to agree upon the relative importance of the virtue concepts within a moral scheme in which notions of rights and utility also have a key place

but also 'an inability to agree upon the content and character of particular virtues'. The notion of virtue here refers to 'a disposition or sentiment which will produce in us obedience to certain rules', but perhaps a better way of identifying this is as values on which we are all agreed, and their relative priorities. I have quoted MacIntyre, not because I agree with his upholding of community and tradition, but because his analysis of a lack of agreed basis in late modern culture is persuasive. However, in the case of family law the conception of justice may be found in the twin values of liberty and equality. The voices that have begun to speak are unlikely to accept silence as the price of community. They are looking for something new. Whereas MacIntyre finds his solution in a return to traditions of exclusion and subordination, to patriarchy and hierarchy, Susan Okin (1989: 60) argues that conversation with such traditions merely convinces the talker that 'there is something fundamentally incoherent about the traditions themselves and that she will have to look elsewhere for answers to questions about justice and rationality'.

The legal response to women, to children, to those with stigmatised identities, and to those coming from other ethnic and religious traditions, has been bitty, leaving us with an incoherent legacy. There has been an expedient response to claims couched in the language of rights, for example, to women's claims for autonomy over their own bodies. Such claims may be successful because the legal tradition is confronted with a clash between its own values and its own tradition. It is notable that, as in the case of the marital rape exemption discussed in Chapter 1, law attempts to uphold values such as liberty and tradition simultaneously, even when they clash. Former court decisions, however unjust they may appear to late moderns, are rarely if ever denounced. Rather, the banal language of 'changed social and economic conditions' is applied as balm to the wound.

What we see and hear in debates about family law today is a struggle over meaning. Whose meaning is to predominate? Is the meaning of marriage to be imposed by law according to Judaeo-Christian tradition? How can justice be given to those whose lives do not fit these meanings, whose values are not reflected in family law, and who are excluded from marriage and parenthood? Exclusion from legal and social institutions may appear voluntary, where it is coercive, as, for example, when the terms of marriage imposed by the state are gender coded, or where one's sexuality excludes one. These are pressing problems which confront the legal culture of the family, and which threaten its fabric. Before, however, we rush to knit up family law's ravelled sleeve of care, we must unpick a seam. Does family law give meaning to our lives that we accept and respect? Or does it stand justly accused as containing the remnants of a tradition that we do not wish to defend? In particular, is the accusation of failure to respect liberty justified?

The Patriarchal Tradition

Once upon a time the authority of husband and father over his family was unquestioned. Although this particular tradition has been questioned and modified in the course of the past 140 years, since judicial divorce was introduced in 1857, it remains with us. If we listen to the story told by Carol Pateman (1988a) we may understand why. This story starts with *Patriarcha*, written by Sir Robert Filmer, a patriarchalist theorist who used the family as a metaphor for political order and understood all relationships of superior and subordinate to be like that of father and son. Through the father the son was subject to the political authority of the monarch. But this attempt to ground political rule in the patriarchal family was rejected by social contract theorists who gave another account which remains influential today.

According to the tale told by the social contract theorists, paternal power was temporary. At the age of maturity sons became as free as their fathers, and government was with their consent. Furthermore, paternal power was distinct from political power. However, in their denial of Filmer's identification of father-right with political right, both Locke and Rousseau forgot that patriarchal power encompassed not only paternal authority but also the legacy of sex-right over wives. Pateman (1988a) argues a failure to distinguish two dimensions of patriarchalism: the paternal and the masculine. She identifies a step in the patriarchal argument that has been overlooked by the social contractarians and their successor theorists. In Filmer's argument sons did not spring up like mushrooms; for fatherly authority to exist a mother had to exist:

> In other words, *sex right or conjugal right must necessarily precede the right of fatherhood* [emphasis in the original, 1988a: 87], and political power lies in the domination of women.

When the sons of Filmer's *Patriarcha* symbolically killed the father in order to enter into the social contract, the wife did not kill the husband. She remained subject to him. In other words, while men were able to free themselves from the old order of status, deference and authority, called patriarchy, women remained subject to it for a longer period. That period is now ending. In building their story on sons, and in ignoring women, the social contractarians hid the original source of political right, namely conjugal right.

The point of Pateman's account for us is that it pins down the political tradition in which family law has grown up. It is hardly surprising then to find difficulties in the location of the family in political theory and of women as civil individuals, or to hear a legal saga such as that of the marital rape exemption. This is not to say that patriarchy is still with us in its original form. It is evident that we have seen and continue to see significant changes in the ways women define themselves and are defined, despite the gender coding that makes up family law. My focus is on the remnants that still go to make up a patchwork of tradition, and that seem to find particular expression where the law deals directly with the relations of women to men. This chapter argues that these remnants remain, in part because of a failure to theorise the family as an institution and its place in the political framework that governs our lives.

For the purposes of this book two aspects of the story of the social contract are particularly relevant. First, there is the lingering legacy in family law of conjugal right and women's location in the private sphere. This leads not only to questions of whether certain values immanent in the law are worth defending, but also to questions about the place of the family in political discourse. With regard to immanent, or embedded, values, these may linger on after the patriarchalism that justified them has been rejected; or there may be traditional values hidden in the law that have not been revealed overtly, but that are no longer shared by many members of the community. Questions about the relationship between the family, civil society and the state arise; the position of the family has not been theorised in political philosophy because it is taken for granted as natural. It is likely that these questions will remain to dislocate family law for the future, particularly if unexamined and untheorised.

Those unconvinced by the above may point to a century and a half of reform, starting with the Matrimonial Causes Act 1857, through the Married Women's Property Acts 1864–82, to the Equal Pay and Sex Discrimination Acts of 1975. They may argue that, whatever the past tradition of family law, we should now go forward. The question to be answered is whether the old political conceptions remain immanent, contained in aspects of law, or whether the tradition in which women were ignored or subordinated has now vanished. This will be developed further in a discussion of citizenship and of the relationship of family and state. But first, the issue of unagreed values will be illustrated by a study of current proposals for divorce law reform. This is to make the point that not only are we haunted by past tradition, but until we have dealt with that, we cannot move forward.

Current Debates and Unagreed Values

'Law claims the power and the ability to translate into its own language all human discourse and action, a necessary precondition for its regulatory function' (Douzinas and Warrington, 1991: ix). But whose discourses, whose ways of seeing, are to be translated? We can make a start with law as the law of the father. Perhaps it was with hypothetical parricide, when the sons of social contract killed off the father, or perhaps it was later with notions of liberty and equality, but law has lost its unquestioned authority. The assumptions, upon which arguments about the content of family law used to be based, have gone. The practice of social criticism means that social institutions, such as family law, require justification in terms of reasons offered. This will be elaborated below, but let us first examine family law's province.

Who is, what is, the self embodied in the law that constitutes and regulates and adjudicates families? In other words, what is the self seen by family law? It has been argued in Chapter 4 that a gendered, heterosexual self is envisaged by marriage law. An incapable self is constituted by child law, as discussed in Chapter 6. But the law goes further in constituting and regulating sexual desire; in saying what is just and fair in marital conduct; in excluding and including relationships under the rubric of family; in benefiting some relationships and not others; in upholding certain traditions, thus embodying particular sorts of selves. Justifying these institutional arrangements with reasons is not easy. The process of justification requires the giving of reasons in universalistic terms, of general applicability, publicly offered and acknowledged.

The MacIntyre (1981) tale of disintegration of community, which leaves us without a moral consensus on which to ground our rules of relationships with others, is nostalgic. Desire for such security may cloud perception of patriarchal values, particular reasons. Those ignored by past tradition may not want to claim it as theirs. Whatever the reasons for communal unravelling it should not be assumed that this process is negative. There can be no ravelling-up of things into the same old shape. Something new will have to be fashioned, if there is to be knitting. The challenge is to make something that takes account of what has been hidden, repressed, silenced, excluded. The current debate on divorce reform patterns the difficulties.

Divorce Law and its Assumptions

Divorce law was last reformed in 1969 (Divorce Reform Act, consolidated in the Matrimonial Causes Act 1973). In the late 1980s the Law Commission undertook a major review and new divorce legislation was proposed (Law Commission, 1988, no 170; 1990, no 192). Whereas the 1969 reforms were discussed extensively with the established church in England, it is noticeable that the 1988 discussion paper is less concerned with the religious reaction. This in itself indicates awareness of fragmentation.

A comparison of the 1966 discussion paper *The Field of Choice* (Law Commission, 1966, no 6), which preceded the 1969 reforms, with the 1988 paper *Facing the Future* (Law Commission, 1988, no 170) reveals the lack of 'shared values' for the later proposed reforms. Whereas the language of the earlier document was concerned with the promotion of the 'stability of marriage, reconciliation, maximum fairness, protection of children and the economically weaker spouse', the 1988 document states that:

> law and practice can no longer be founded on the assumption that people affected by divorce are a small and deviant proportion of the population. Secondly, the 'consumer interest' in both the substantive and procedural aspects of the divorce law is proportionately that much greater and must be taken into account in any evaluation of the present law or proposals for reform. (1988, no 170, para 2.22)

Thus the debate has shifted from idealised standards and a confident morality, to consumer-led opinions and efficiency as the standard of justice.

Gradual fragmentation, over 22 years, of the community idealised by philosophers such as MacIntyre may be deduced from textual comparison of the two documents; or the hypothesis may be advanced that the earlier apparent consensus was imposed. The language of 1966 contained humanitarian values. There was talk of 'maximum fairness, and the minimum bitterness, distress and humiliation' (1966, no 6, para 15), of decency and dignity. The language of 1988 is of efficiency, pragmatism and resignation. For example, at an early stage it is acknowledged that the reforms of 1969 led to procedures which 'were often unnerving and humiliating for the petitioner'; that there was 'a rapid escalation of legal aid expenditure on divorce'; that 'registrars act as little more than "rubber stamps"'; that there is 'no adequate system for checking whether the petitioner has proved the contents of the petition' (Law Commission, 1988, paras 2.6, 2.8). The subtext of this last point is that the system is open to abuse and perjury. This leaves the ground open for a move to less surveillance by the courts of the termination of marriage.

Of particular interest is the discussion of 'fault'. One of the jewels in the crown of the common law is its procedures for ascertaining truth, allocating fault, responsibility and blame. A trial, whether civil or criminal, is designed to establish the facts, apply the law, draw conclusions, and produce a result – a fine, a not-guilty verdict, compensation for a wrong. A trial is a recreation of 'what happened', with blame for those at fault. This was the method applied to family law in its ecclesiastical origins, and in its judicial phase from 1857. Doubts about the suitability of this method of inquiry for marital termination are now instated. In 1966 there was some discussion of the limits of judicial inquiry into the breakdown of marriage. Whereas the Archbishop of Canterbury's Group, convened to discuss the established church's views on divorce law reform, had published a report entitled *Putting Asunder* (1966) in which it favoured court adjudication of marriage breakdown, this was officially rejected by the Law Commission in the same year on the grounds that breakdown was not a justiciable issue. However, the notion of fault, which had previously dominated divorce law was retained in relation to 'adultery' and 'behaviour', two 'facts' which could be elicited as evidence of breakdown. In other words, fault was retained, and with it law's claims to establish truth and blame. Fault gave the prospect of a quick divorce, as other non-fault-based 'facts' required a minimum wait of two years. The point of this discussion is that the 1988 text admits that law's ability 'to conduct a proper inquiry' (Law Commission, 1988, no 170, para 2.8) into irretrievable breakdown of marriage is strictly limited; and the 1990 document says that the courts are capable of assessing marital fault only 'in the crudest possible way' (Law Commission, 1990, no 192, para 3.6). Thus, law's claim to establish 'truth' in divorce cases has been abandoned. Although this is justified in terms of encouraging 'the parties to look to the future rather than to dwell in the past' (Law Commission, 1988, no 170, para 3.3) the significance of the abandonment of this site should not be overlooked. It is part of the retreat of family law from an overt moral discourse, because the notion of shared, or imposed, values is being abandoned. However, it seems that policy makers are reluctant to abandon completely their claim to make 'a coherent and consistent moral law' (Law Commission, 1990, no 192, para 3.40); and such perspectives remain embedded in family law in the wider sense.

The 1988 document, while criticising the 1966 text, is an indictment of the present divorce law. It may also be read as placing the limits to law's powers in human relationships. The Divorce Reform Act 1969 is held up as having failed to perform the humanitarian tasks of ensuring the stability of marriages while destroying the 'empty shell' of those that are dead, promoting 'maximum fairness' with 'minimum bitterness, distress and humiliation' (Law Commission, 1988, no 170, para 2.3). This indictment, which is supported by considerable empirical research, enables the Law Commission to move to its own preferred solution, presented in terms of consumer choice, efficiency and pragmatism. Justice is now defined in terms of procedure rather than substance. Underlying the 1988 text is resignation, a retreat from the earlier confidences of 1966 in the essential goodness or even perfectibility of man.

The retreat identified may be welcomed as making way for pluralism. But it takes place in the name of pragmatism and not liberty. Thus 'virtually any spouse can assemble a list of events, which taken out of context, can be presented as unreasonable behaviour sufficient to found a divorce petition' (Law Commission, 1988, no 170, para 3.8). An adultery petition is an 'easy option' for 'determined parties' (1988, no 170, para 3.8), who may perjure themselves (1988, no 170, paras

3.45, 5.16). Not only are consumers manipulating the law, but it is not possible to allocate blame as in 'most divorces the spouses will both be "at fault" in varying degrees' (1988, no 170, para 3.16). And the legal process may itself be 'such as to provoke or exacerbate unnecessary antagonism between parties' (1988, no 170, para 3.22).

One of the values of a good divorce law, according to the Law Commission, is fairness. The present law is seen as unfair and as exacerbating bitterness and hostility; so it is the legal divorce 'system' which engenders conflict (Law Commission, 1988, no 170, para 3.41). The elimination of fault and of consensual divorce, where the spouse who least wishes to divorce is given an 'unfair advantage in negotiations about children, finances and property' (1988, no 170, para 5.18), will lead to the avoidance of the unfair stigmatisation of one party. Fairness, then, is to be realised by leaving divorce to be worked out as 'a process over time' (1988, no 170, para 5.22). Law's aspirations in divorce are to be limited. Enter then the figure of the respondent to a 'behaviour' petition who has 'been guilty of violence or other forms of serious misconduct'. While 'undeserving of sympathy' (1988, no 170, para 3.27), the bringing out of such behaviour in public, the paper says, will not reduce conflict. It may further upset the children. Thus ideas about justice, in the sense of a public hearing and condemnation of conduct that falls below a certain standard, are no longer considered appropriate to family law. What we are seeing is judicial and professional awareness of law's limitations as a means of social control, particularly where values are unagreed. The research evidence of courts' reluctance to become involved in tricky or sticky family disputes already exists (Davis, 1987). However, the reader should not necessarily conclude that this is merely a family law problem with no relevance to other areas of law.

The quotations from the Law Commission documents above are designed to illustrate the extent to which legal policy makers are abandoning law's claims to knowledge and judgment of human domestic behaviour. For example, although children are traumatised by divorce, there are said to be cases in which this is still the best course for them, but 'others in which it is impossible to tell which course will be best' (1988, no 170, para 3.37). The epistemological consequences of the abandonment of the claim to know are significant. A lack of confidence about the values that the law should uphold is also evident. It might be argued that, whatever the reasons for a retreat from judgment, liberty will be increased by law's retreat. This is a consequentialist argument, possibly susceptible to empirical confirmation, but only after the fact. However, the reasons for law's proposed abandonment of the epistemological high ground are not couched in terms of liberty. This value has not been discussed by the Law Commission; rather the concern is pragmatic. Procedural issues, costs, efficiency,

rationing of legal services: these are important concerns of the administration of justice. But this must not obscure from us the retreat from
proud confidence.

Truths and Knowledges

'The complexities of family life are no longer capable of being reduced
to simple certainties' (Law Commission, 1990, no 190, para 3.6). This
chapter is concerned with law's abandonment of claims to knowledge.
Although the claim to have procedures for establishing truth may be
retained in other areas of law, and family law may be dismissed as inappropriate to legal method, we are witnessing a new development.
More general epistemological doubts have been expressed about legislation regulating divorce. Ruth Deech (1990: 229) points out that the
empirical material which grounded the reforms of divorce law in the
1960s 'led to wholly inaccurate predictions and that there is no reason
to suppose that the 1988 effort is any more reliable'. Although this might
be interpreted as a call for better research or more accurate facts,
Deech's call is for a return to precedent and principle as protective of
civil liberties, to judicial administration as upholder of legal standards.
Scepticism over claims to knowledge, particularly those based on small
empirical samples, have been expressed in other quarters.

Poststructuralists challenge the findings about a 'real world' out
there waiting to be discovered (Douzinas and Warrington, 1991). Not
only are the methods of research, the questions asked and the conclusions drawn under suspicion (Eekelaar and Maclean, 1990), but
doubts go to the very categories of construction such as 'woman' or
'man'. Knowledge begets knowledge, but refers back to what is already
known. What is unseen, unspoken, unheard, unthought, undefined,
cannot be known. Thus, for example, physical and sexual abuse of less
powerful family members has only recently been 'discovered'. The claim
to knowledge, on which 'experts' live, is double-faced. It may enable
the discovery of new victims of domestic tyranny or new crimes. But
it may also enable the creation of new subjects/objects of professional
practices and surveillance.

According to the Law Commission (1990, no 192, para 2.11) current
divorce law pretends that the court is conducting an inquiry into
truth, but this is false. Furthermore it is difficult 'to get at the truth in
an undefended case'. The scepticism over realism may be shared, but
prescriptions differ. Ruth Deech believes in a world of legal autonomy
with principles and standards, legal procedures and methods, a world
where the legal system has faith in itself, uncontaminated by external
viewpoints. Poststructuralists offer criticism of procedures, plurality of
principles, scepticism of unitary standards, rejection of law's power.

Examples given by Deech in support of her argument concern false predictions before the 1969 reforms on the number of children born outside marriage, the use of fault-based divorce which generated hypocrisy, and the general rate of divorce, all of which were expected to fall. Instead the unpredicted happened, and the policies justifying the reforms now seem wrong. Where predicated on some notion of 'social cure' these policies represent a failure of understanding of change. Doubts must arise concerning any direct connection between the ways people organise their lives and legal provisions. Thus arguments about 'reality' lose their power. But this is not an argument for the retention of tradition; rather it is an argument about unpredictability or inability to predict in social research. It also undermines confident claims to know. Therefore a family law that values liberty and equality might be a more appropriate way of dealing with lack of knowledge.

We can relate this discussion to what was earlier said about a lack of an agreed basis for family law. It now seems that not only do we lack an agreed basis for the law but we also cannot claim to know what is wanted, even by 'consumers'. Predictions of effects and consequences, or people's behaviour, must be treated sceptically. In short, we know little of what has happened and nothing of the future. What is evident is that family law in its constitutive and regulatory aspects proceeds on assumptions about a person, an individual, a self, who is a construct of particular imaginings.

The Selves Constituted in Family Law

Family law operates on a gendered self, despite the gender neutrality of its language, as we have already noted in Chapter 5. The child as a self is almost entirely absent, as noted in Chapter 6, being object not subject. But is there a level of generality at which the adult selves come together as ungendered beings? In other words, is family law susceptible to interpretation as a universal norm applicable to all adults? If so, what type of self is projected: the sober, calculating, rational man beloved of the market, or a feeling, connected woman described by relational moralists, such as Gilligan (1982)? In so forming the question there is danger of falling into the dichotomous form of argument so prevalent and yet so criticised in common law reasoning. The point is to approach the issue of values, of embedded moralities, from another angle of the camera.

Law is theorised by Judith Grbich (1991: 67) as imaginary or creative language 'expressive of embodied practices of situated experience or of subjective life'. She advocates engagement with those practices that appear to have excluded women's imaginings of life possibilities from the conversations of 'humanity', and inquiry 'into the ways in which legal reasoning transforms the embodied imaginings into the "objective" form of doctrine which passes for the "normative"' (1991: 69). The point of this reference to Grbich is that she posits a legal self produced by male imaginings – presumably as law makers, decision takers, rule administrators. Such a self *can be* gendered as female or male but is a product of male imagination. It is nevertheless worth pursuing these embodied imaginings to identify what kinds of being, of construct, they are.

In the discourse of divorce law reform already analysed we find figures of consumers looking for an efficient way out of their marriages, of sensitive persons who may feel angry and humiliated at the unfairness of a law which stigmatises them in divorce petitions as violent and unreasonable, of a bitter post-divorce person who 'may feel so resentful that he wants to cut himself off entirely from what has happened and so loses contact with his children' (Law Commission, 1988, no 170, para 3.41). Largely suppressed is the violence and physical abuse that accompanies too many marriages.

As shown in Chapter 5, maternal and paternal selves are construed differently: the former as specialist in affection, child care and domesticity; the latter as specialist in the labour market and discipline. The possibilities of constructions seem to be various, and the gendered nature of family law leads to the conclusion that the domestic sphere is where gendered persons cohabit and that there is no transcendental ungendered self. Marriage is the primary social paradigm of a gender relationship, despite law's efforts at gender neutrality. When we think marriage, we think gender. But do the genders engendered by family law have any correspondence in the persons or identities of those subject to law?

If family law assumes a gendered person, other branches of law are predicated on a universal individual. For example, criminal law uses the standard of the 'reasonable man' to determine a range of questions about appropriate responses to physical threats. That this legal construct might mask a gendered individual has only recently been appreciated. Thus abused women who respond to violence in a legally inappropriate manner may find their actions termed 'unreasonable', although their gender may inhibit them from the legally understood response. The legal defence of provocation, which enables the reduction of a crime from homicide to manslaughter, requires 'a sudden and temporary loss of self-control'. It has been argued that such a quick loss of temper may be unavailable to a woman when abused by a man of whom she is afraid or who is more powerful than she is (O'Donovan, 1991). The point is not to advocate the entry of more gendered persons into law as subjects. It is to point out that a so-called universal subject may mask a gendered subject, thus denying equality under the law to those whose ways of being are unrecognised.

In political discourse, in political theory, in law directly concerned with subjects of the state, an ungendered subject is assumed. The challenge issued by theorists such as Okin (1989) and Pateman (1988a, b) is that this subject is male. In their view political theory has performed the trick of smuggling men only into seemingly portman-teau language. If this charge can be sustained, it is serious; for the function of political discourse is to justify political institutions. In a democracy such as Britain this is done through claims about equality under the law. Gender, then, is a slippery substance. It enters into family law overtly, and into public law and criminal law covertly. It remains for this writer an open question as to whether the notion of a universal subject can be sustained, or whether gender will inevitably effect entryism. To understand this latter point the feminist challenge to the place of the family in political theory requires further elaboration. We can then see whether the ideal of citizenship is susceptible to devel-opment in terms that include all persons under the umbrella of 'universal'.

Family and Citizenship for All as Equals?

The zones occupied by families and by citizens in the structure of society are different. In traditional political theory there are three levels: family, civil society and state. Citizenship, as a concept, relates to the state, although citizens may act together in civil society, and spring from families. Children, by definition, are not citizens. By reason of nonage they are deemed incapable of performing acts such as voting, repre-senting, contracting, engaging with law – acts which mark both the adult and the citizen. However incoherent law's position on children and their emancipation, it is confident in its denial of citizenship to this group. As demonstrated in Chapter 6, there are differing ages which render lawful activities such as consent to marriage, to medical treatment, to heterosexual intercourse, to male homosexual acts, whereas 18 is the age of emancipation, being a full legal subject, citi-zenship. A developmental approach to children's maturity, observable in some aspects of criminal law and family law, is a recognition of sub-jectivity. But whereas male children will enter freely into full capacity on reaching the ages of 18, or 21 for sexual choice, women, it is argued cannot do so because their choices are restricted.

According to Carole Pateman (1988b: 114), women are outwith the social contract – and therefore political society – in two senses; they are:

> excluded from an agreement through which the brothers inherit their legacy of patriarchal sex right and legitimize their claim over women's bodies and ability to give birth.

Furthermore, civil law is agreed self-governance by men, restraining their desires, applying equally to them all. But women are outside this agreement, having been defined as incapable of reason, a quality required for entry. Thus:

> the patriarchal claim that there is a 'foundation in nature' for women's subjection to men is a claim that women's bodies must be governed by men's reason. (Pateman, 1988b: 115)

A major question is whether Pateman's argument is about an essentialist aspect of political society, or about an historical and contingent social legacy. Her argument supports the claim that law is made by men as a projection of their own fears and desires. Women are there only in male imaginings. If that is so, then such gendered law as purports to be about women, and such universal law as purports to be about adults, represent male projections of their ideas of what women are, or of what a legal subject is. The legacy of the place of the family in the social structure must then be affected by patriarchy. But even if Pateman is said to be addressing history, the political tradition that excluded women and the family cannot easily be brushed aside. Adding women and stirring is not open to theorists who continue to use the old ingredients. And, as the language of adding women and stirring suggests, pushing something new into old forms is a non-recognition of the shape of what is new. To continue the cookery analogy, the new ingredient may interact with the old to produce something inedible, or even poisonous, to all.

Political theory is about justifying political institutions that are coercive and non-voluntary. Reasons for excluding the family from political conversations may call on the notion that the natural (family) is not political. Counter arguments point to the social character of family and political institutions. The family is coercive in the sense that we have no choice concerning our births, in terms of whether, why, when, what sex, what race, what nationality, what culture, or to whom. The social meaning attached to race, sex (gender), class is likewise not a matter of individual choice. It seems to me that it is right to ask for justification in terms of general reasons of social arrangements which are non-voluntary. The distinction made between the natural and the political does not hold up. Family law as a social institution cannot be above social criticism, particularly where it relies on a feature which is ascriptive and non-voluntary, such as sex, to justify its practices. In terms of political theory the gender order requires justification.

This chapter started with the problem of the lack of an agreed basis for family law decisions and legislation. Patriarchy lingers on in various ways – in the gendered basis of court decisions, in attitudes, and in the values immanent in the law. This last point means that, if the family law tradition is called on to deal with difficult or new issues, patriarchy re-surfaces. But moving on to new forms of analysis or solution is impeded by lack of agreement. The question of the place of the family in the social structure is an example of disagreement not only on the level of political theory but also at the level of practice. This is important because it is only through conversation about the relationship between family and social structure that the possibility of putting patriarchy behind us can be realised. For this conversation to be justified it must allow people of all kinds, backgrounds and ages to speak.

A major question is whether theorisation of the family brings it into the political arena, as an aspect of civil society; or whether the family can be theorised as separate from civil society and ideas of citizenship. Susan Okin (1989, Ch. 8) has proposed a family which remains in a separate sphere from citizenship, but to which principles of justice are applied. She is not convinced of Pateman's argument that theories built around the notion of individuals who contract necessarily assume the subjection of women (Okin, 1990: 659). Furthermore, the issue of how to organise life 'in a society that completely rejected both contract and the notion of the liberal individual' (1990: 668) remains for Okin. Getting rid of the gendered basis of family relations is her view of what justice requires. This is an attempt to bring some notion of universality, based on contract as a justification, to the political theory of the family.

Okin's Just Family

'Most [theorists] seem to think that just men spring like mushrooms from the earth.' Thus Okin (1989: 21) indicts political philosophy. Her analysis has two parts: a deconstruction of the traditional, unjust, gendered family order; a reconstruction of the family according to principles of justice elaborated by John Rawls (1971) whereby a social contract would enter the family. Okin's deconstructive analysis points to two presumptions central to the socially created unequal division of labour: that women are primarily responsible for the rearing of children; that serious members of the workforce do not have child-care responsibilities. The family is a school of injustice, in which children see that gender-structured marriage makes women socially and economically vulnerable, but may take this as given, accepting it unquestioningly as natural or as part of the gender order. What, then, Okin asks, are future citizens to learn of fairness, of nurturing, of the value of domestic work? But 'justice is a virtue of fundamental importance for families, as for other basic social institutions ... a sphere of life that is absolutely crucial to moral development'(1989: 135). What is striking in Okin's analysis is that she brings out the effect on children's sense of justice of living in gendered, and therefore unfair, homes, thus crystallising the habitual neglect of the family by other theorists. To deal with this she proposes a genderless family, of equal sharing of parenting and wages, equally shared roles. For couples who prefer the previous tradition, she proposes that the earnings of the market participant belong equally to both. This is linked into John Rawls's contractarian theory of justice by the argument that this type of arrangement would be chosen by gender-blind persons in the 'original position', that is, choosing the principles of justice without knowledge of their own actual positions. Rawls uses this device as a sort of mind experiment whereby we are asked to choose just principles from behind a 'veil of ignorance', thus precluding a mere counting of heads and, possibly, dominance.

Genderlessness for Okin means that no social or legal significance would be attached in her ideal world to the ascriptive quality of sex, other than in relation to maternity. She does not propose, as some have done, that the gestation and birth of children be untied from sex and removed to an artificial womb. For Okin's idea to work the persons choosing genderlessness as the just principle for families must either stem from a genderless society, or be risk averse, or have imaginative sympathy. By this I mean that it must first be appreciated that present family arrangements, based on gender, are unjust; and that therefore no rational person would choose a gender-ordered society. Liberal philosophy is built on the assumption that individuals are self-interested. Rawls (1972) designs his hypothetical original position, in which the principles of justice are chosen behind a 'veil of ignorance', to take account of this basic supposition. In other words, we are denied information about ourselves in order to ask us what principles we would countenance if we did not know our lot. Okin assumes that the present gender order would be overthrown, because men would fear ending up as women. To suffer from such fear a man would have to see a gender-ordered society as unjust; to feel that being a man is preferable to being a woman. It is not self-evident that this perception is general among most men and some women. So it seems that the burden of proof remains with those who argue that a gendered family order is unfair.

In *Justice, Gender and the Family* (1989), Okin faces the objections that the self projected in Rawls's scheme is egotistic and individualistic; and that it aims to create a universalistic and impartial set of principles which leads to the neglect of otherness or difference (1989: 100). To defend Rawls from these criticisms Okin is forced to introduce the idea of empathy:

Those in the original position cannot think from the position of *nobody*, as is suggested by those critics who then conclude that Rawls's theory depends upon a 'disembodied' concept of the self. They must, rather, think from the perspective of *everybody*, in the sense of *each in turn*. To do this requires at least strong empathy and a pre-paredness to listen carefully to the very different points of view of others. (1989: 101)

Although Rawls uses the language of forcing the individual to take others into account, it is in terms of a rational choice because one does not know what kind of self one will turn out to be. This is not empathy, nor does Rawls require it; rather he deliberately creates a hypothetical original position in which it is unnecessary.

Aside from the questions raised by her introduction of empathy, Okin also faces the issue of the rational choosing person. The representative human beings, she says, 'must be persons whose psychological and moral development is in all essentials identical' (1989: 107). The only way to produce such persons is through genderless institutions and customs. Only when men nurture and women take part 'in what have been principally men's realms', will 'members of both sexes be able to develop a more complete *human* personality than has hitherto been possible' (1989: 107). It seems therefore that a genderless society must precede the original position, for presently constituted human beings are inadequate to choose principles of justice. They have been educated in gendered families to accept the present order as natural and inevitable. Transcending the handicaps of one's upbringing may not be possible.

It is not clear that Rawls can be adapted to bring justice to the family. But this does not render Okin's project otiose. In particular her points about limited conceptions of justice which result from the raising of children in an unjust, gendered system are well made. But this is precisely what leads to complacency among some men and women over the current gender order. One disappointment is that Okin does not broach the issue of justice to the children themselves. As we saw in Chapter 5, the denial of legal status to children as legal subjects may lead to injustice. Just as abusing parents are said to turn their children into abusers, it may be that being the object of injustice makes one unjust to one's own children. One's sense of justice is developed by the treatment one receives in addition to the treatment of others that one witnesses. Okin says that the example of the traditional family is a school of injustice, because of the way that wives and mothers are subordinated, but there is also the example of how the children themselves are treated, which she omits. These examples of unjust treatment may be internalised and become so pervasive a part of self-conception and how the world is conceived that the injustice is not apparent to individuals. This does not make the family any less unjust. On the contrary, it may make it more so, not only because those who receive injustice perpetuate it, but also because they and their children are denied a means of analysing, of seeing, the just and the unjust.

In a review of Okin, Kymlicka (1991) points to issues that remain undiscussed. Who has the right to form a family, to bear children, to parent? Before we talk of equal parenting by adults of both sexes

(Okin, 1989: 100), we need to determine a theory of family justice, which might look radically different from Okin's version, otherwise we are accepting the old ideology of the natural heterosexual family, and merely redistributing its tasks. Furthermore, genuine genderlessness is not necessarily limited to the equal mothering and fathering advocated by Okin, but might encompass parenting by any persons or group so desiring. It seems that Okin is willing to go a certain distance with the idea of contract as the basis for family life, but shrinks from what Pateman (1988a: 184) has called 'the logic of contract' in 'a universal market in bodies and services'. Kymlicka (1991: 94) thinks that 'the real reason people object to commodifying reproduction and sex ... is that it is "dehumanizing" or "alienating"'. In his view this argument could be carried against freedom of contract in general; and, further, it is 'not available to a liberal – it belongs to the vocabulary of perfectionism, which liberal neutrality disavows' (1991: 96). Perhaps, therefore, the reason why political theorists have avoided theorising the family, and have placed it in the realm of the natural or the sacred, is that they would otherwise be confronted with the logic of commodification, if they belong to the liberal tradition. Whether the logic of contract leading to a market in bodies, organs and babies illustrates the limited usefulness of liberalism, as Pateman thinks, or whether notions of justice within liberal theory will act as a brake on such a market, as Okin thinks, remains in debate.

To sum up so far: Pateman indicts the full tradition of political theory, although whether she should be interpreted as denying the possibility of a future free individual in a non-patriarchal society is not evident. Okin hopes to adapt social contractarian ideas to the family and thereby to offer a way out. One thing is clear: there is no going back to an untheorised family. The challenge is to practise social criticism; that is, to put the family as an institution to the test of justificatory discussion, and to fashion something new if present arrangements are unjust. This is where the idea of family law as conversation plays a part. If we value liberty and equality, how are we to go forward? Faced with this difficulty, the recent answer in relation to family law has been retreat from overt conversation about values. But the state cannot escape so easily. It must justify its laws, particularly those restricting liberty, denying equality, or stigmatising persons and relationships; it must stand for certain beliefs; it must legitimise social institutions and practices. However, since doing so will remove the family from the realm of the natural, or the sacred, the reluctance is understandable.

It is not only a question of justifying family laws and the gender order – if retained; it is also a question of theorising the relationship of the family to other political institutions. Again, assumptions about the family have precluded this work in mainstream theory. To conclude this chapter we must further consider family and citizenship.

Citizenship as a Universal Ideal and its Relationship to Family

This book has already argued that current family laws are unfair, excluding those who want to create family relationships but are denied the legal capacity to do so, perpetuating an unfair sex/gender system, educating children in injustice. By comparison, the ideal of citizenship is of neutrality and universality – a conversation in which particular identities and experiences are left behind and a general perspective is adopted. This might be achievable if something like Okin's genderless family develops. But what passes for universal must be genuinely so; otherwise, universal citizenship will repeat past experiences of being 'incorporated' into the body politic for those excluded.

Given the differentiation of society, and the differences among persons, we have to be careful about ideas of the universal. There are some problems here for law, which claims its authority from its general applicability. Scepticism about the generality of present family law has been a feature of this book, even when seeming universality is under discussion. The fragmentation of identity which characterises the late modern period increases the difficulties of generalisation. From this follows doubts about a universal, portmanteau self as the citizen, or as the legal individual.

The idea of family law as conversation is intended to bring together citizenship, where persons voice their concerns and beliefs, and family membership, where most of us live. It is sometimes proposed that citizenship should include an obligation of abstraction: a stepping outside one's individual concerns and seeing one's point of view as one among many; a juxtaposing of other points of view. This is what conversation does. The difficulty is that each person is assumed capable of the virtue of empathy and the judgement of Portia. Putting self-interest aside becomes the mark of the citizen. Those who have been traditionally urged to do so in the family may be suspicious, as often the self-sacrifice demanded was asymmetrical. And who is to judge among the various viewpoints, empathy notwithstanding?

An additional step in the effort to retain universality is to a collective sphere of justification in which actions can be challenged, when an infringement of liberty or equality is in question, even though this takes place in private or stems from a personal belief. Such a breach in the traditional separation of spheres might ensure a standard within the family that can be justified in the public realm. This is one way of dealing with the thorny issues of personal belief and behaviour in the domestic sphere. It also moves the discussion away from court-centredness to a political forum. Anne Phillips (1991: 85) argues that there should be certain aspects of our lives that we are entitled to treat as private, such as our sexual lives, but that:

we should also be entitled to demonstrate publicly on all sexual issues, and none should be excluded from public discussion as inappropriate or trivial or better suited to the private domain.

The central problem in family law identified at the beginning of this chapter as a lack of an agreed basis for legislation and decision making would be open to conversation. Present conceptions of the family as sacred, natural and beyond discussion should be opened up in such conversations. Values, whether traditional or egalitarian, are an important focus of discussion. The theorising of the family, so necessary for understanding, might then follow.

End Thoughts

This book set out to identify points of view generally omitted from writings about family law. As a book of perspectives it also acknowledges the active role of writers and readers in the construction of knowledge. It is true that the power we have is not comparable to that of judge, legislator or administrator. Yet what and how we think, and our reflections on how we think, are significant. I have identified my position as that of an outsider, one who takes up a position external to legal institutions governing the family and examines them from there. I do not claim that mine is a view from nowhere. The standards against which I have consistently evaluated family law are those of liberty and equality. I am aware that conceptions of these virtues may clash and that others upholding them may disagree with me. But I do not think that those others will be able to claim to uphold certain institutional aspects of English family law as it exists today while concurrently claiming to speak for justice.

The qualities of generality and accessibility have long been held to be an essential part of the rule of law, as has the ideal of equality under the law. If family law denies access to marriage to persons because of their particular sexual attachments, does it matter? If entry into marriage is culturally coded, if the conditions of the relationship itself are controlled by law and gender coded, then general justifications may reasonably be sought. If these cannot be found in language consonant with law's own standards of justice, of the rule of law, then something is wrong. And it matters.

The idea of the series in which this book appears is to bring out what is suppressed in standard texts, and I have tried to do so. Inevitably, then, the focus is on the excluded: children, homosexuals, but also heterosexuals of both sexes. For this is one odd conclusion. Current family law restricts the freedom of all of us. It does so in different ways, and the consequences are more serious for some. It is self-evident that law restricts. This is its job. But does it need to restrict us in the ways it does at present? Must it construct us as objects, as gendered, as stigmatised? Must it tell men what it means to be masculine, privileging but limiting them in myriad ways? I think not.

An advantage of the outsider vantage point is that one has a distance that is not obtainable by the insider. Furthermore, the insider is concerned with institutional details, with how the pieces of law fit together, with what appears possible in doctrinal terms, with the maintenance of tradition and continuity. For the outsider these aspects of legal institutions may be useful as explanations for why things are the way they are, but not as justifications. The idea of justification must relate to what is just, what can be justified, to justice. Yet the insider/outsider viewpoints do get mixed up, often in law teaching, where I believe they should be kept separate. The marital rape exemption, the story of which helped at the outset of this book, illustrates again. The issue of the exemption has been in debate among law teachers and practitioners since I first started teaching family law in England in 1974. Colleagues seriously concerned with ideas of justice assured me on regular occasions that abolition of the exemption was not possible because of difficulties of evidence, proof, and because of the dangers of misuse by vindictive wives. Their viewpoint was internal, and possibly limited in other ways. But justice is not the preserve of lawyers and teachers. It belongs to us all. Justification must be from viewpoints external to legal institutions. And it must be in terms of standards such as equality, liberty, friendship, empathy.

My open espousal of the virtues of liberty and equality throughout this book does not signify an unthinking stance, or vapid use of language. As my final chapter shows, I anticipate disagreement about what these virtues require. But the first task is to bring the family out of the realm of the natural, the sacred, the holy. By this I mean that the first task is to theorise the family. Just as the state, once holy, with its authority linked to a deity, has been politically justified, so too must that nuclear unit we call the family be theorised. When this happens, I believe that the institutional explanations for current family law will be revealed as lacking foundations in the language of justice.

Justice, as I have said, belongs to everyone. It is not exclusive. We must listen to the voices of those excluded by past practices, excluded from being, excluded from knowing, excluded from participation, excluded by law or by politics. And when all the voices have been heard, and when the choices are made, we must be ready to justify what the law is in terms of external standards which relate to conceptions of justice.

Katherine O'Donovan
Florence
2 May 1992

References

Abel, R., 1988, *The Legal Profession in England and Wales*, Blackwell.

Allen, H., 1987, *Justice Unbalanced*, Open University Press.

Archbold, 1822, *Pleading and Evidence*, London.

Aries, P., 1962, *Centuries of Childhood*, Jonathan Cape.

Aries, P., 1977, 'The Family and the City', in A. Rossi et al. (eds) *The Family*, Norton.

Aries, P. and Duby P. (eds) 1987–1990, *A History of Private Life*, 4 vols, Harvard University Press.

Atiyah, P., 1983, *Law and Modern Society*, Oxford University Press.

Atkins, S. and Hoggett, B., 1984, *Women and the Law*, Blackwell.

Bainham, A., 1990, 'The Privatisation of the Public Interest in Children', *Modern Law Review*, vol 53, p 206.

Bankowski, Z. and Mungham, G., 1976, *Images of Law*, Routledge.

Barrett, M. and McIntosh, M., 1982, *The Anti-Social Family*, New Left Books.

Bennett, B., 1991, 'The Economics of Wifing Services: Law and Economics on the Family', *Journal of Law and the Family*, vol 18, p 206.

Blackstone, W., 1765, *Commentaries on the Law of England*, London.

Bradley, D., 1987, 'Homosexuality and Child Custody in English Law', *International Journal of Law and the Family*, vol 1, p 155.

Bradley, D., 1990, 'Radical Principles and the Legal Institution of Marriage: Domestic Relations Law and Social Democracy in Sweden', *International Journal of Law and the Family*, vol 4, p 206.

Bradney, A., 1979, 'The Family in Family Law', *Family Law*, vol 9, p 244.

Brooks, R., 1989, 'Marital Consent in Rape', *Criminal Law Review*, p 877.

Brophy, J., 1985, 'Child Care and the Growth of Power', in J. Brophy and C. Smart (eds) *Women in Law*, Routledge.

Brophy, J., and Smart C., 1985, 'Locating Law: A Discussion of the Place of Law in Feminist Politics', in J. Brophy and C. Smart (eds) *Women in Law*, Routledge.

Brown, Sir S., 1990, 'Reform and the Rise of Family Law', *Holdsworth Club*, University of Birmingham.

Burgoyne, J., Ormrod, and Richards, M., 1987, *Divorce Matters*, Penguin.

Campbell, B., 1980, 'A Feminist Sexual Politics', *Feminist Review*, vol 5, p 1.

Carlen, P. and Worrall, A., 1987, *Gender, Crime and Justice*, Open University Press.

Carty, A. and Mair, J., 1990, 'Some Post-Modern Perspectives on Law and Society', *Journal of Law and Society*, vol 17, p 395.

Central Statistics Office, 1991, *Social Trends, 22*, HMSO.

Chapman R. and Rutherford, J. (eds) 1988, *Male Order: Unwrapping Masculinity*, Lawrence and Wishart.

Children Come First, 1990, White Paper, Cmnd 1264, 2 vols, HMSO.

Chitty, 1834, *Treatise on Medical Jurisprudence*, London.

Chodorow, N., 1978, *The Reproduction of Mothering: Psychoanalysis and the Sociology of Mothering*, University of California Press.

Collier, R., 1991a, 'Masculinism, Law and Law Teaching', *International Journal of the Sociology of Law*, vol 19, p 427.

Collier, R., 1991b, *'The Art of Living the Married Life: Representations of Heterosexuality in Law'*, unpublished paper, University of Newcastle upon Tyne.

Cover, R., 1986, 'Violence and The Word', *Yale Law Journal*, vol 95, p 1601.

Crane, P., 1982, *Gays and the Law*, Pluto Press.

Criminal Law Revision Committee, 1980, *Working Party on Sexual Offences*, HMSO.

Crisp, Q., 1986, *The Naked Civil Servant*, Jonathan Cape.

Davis, G., 1987, 'Public Issues and Private Troubles: The Case of Divorce', *Family Law*, vol 17, p 299.

Davis, G. and Murch, M., 1988, *Grounds for Divorce*, Oxford University Press.

De Crow, K., 1983, *Sexism and the Law*.

Deech, R., 1990, 'Divorce Law and Empirical Studies', *Law Quarterly Review*, vol 106, p 229.

Dennish, N., Henriques, F. and Slaughter, 1969, *Coal Is Our Life*, Tavistock.

Dewar, J., 1989, *Law and the Family*, Butterworth.

Dingwall, R., Eekelaar, J. and Murray, T., 1983, *The Protection of Children*, Blackwell.

Donzelot, J., 1979, *The Policing of Families*, Hutchinson.

Douzinas, C. and Warrington, R., 1991, '"A Well-Founded Fear of Justice": Law and Ethics in Postmodernity', *Law and Critique*, vol 2, p 115.

Douzinas, C. and Warrington, R., with S. McVeigh, 1991, *Postmodern Jurisprudence: The Law of Test in the Texts of Law*, Routledge.

East, 1805, *Pleas of the Crown*, London.

Eaton, M., 1986, *Justice for Women? Family, Court and Social Control*, Open University Press.

Eekelaar, J., 1978, *Family Law and Social Policy*, Weidenfeld and Nicholson.

Eekelaar, J., 1984, *Family Law and Social Policy*, 2nd edn, Weidenfeld and Nicholson.

Eekelaar, J., 1989, 'What Is Critical About Family Law?', *Law Quarterly Review*, vol 105, p 144.

Eekelaar, J., Clive, E., Clarke, K. and Raikes, S., 1977, *Custody After Divorce*, Centre for Sociolegal Studies, Oxford.

Eekelaar, J. and Maclean, M., 1990, 'Divorce Law and Empirical Studies – A Reply', *Law Quarterly Review*, vol 106, p 621.

Elshtain, J., 1981, *Public Man, Private Woman*, Princeton University Press.

Elshtain, J. (ed) 1982, *The Family in Political Thought*, Harvester.

Farmer, L., 1989, 'Recognising Marital Rape', *SCOLAG*, no 146, p 102.

Filmer, R., 1949, *Patriarcha* (P. Laslett ed), Blackwell.

Foucault, M., 1979, *Discipline and Punish*, Vintage Books.

Foucault, M., 1980, *Power/Knowledge*, Pantheon Books.

Foucault, M., 1981, *The History of Sexuality*, vol 1 (R. Hurley, trans), Penguin.

Foucault, M., 1988, *Technologies of the Self*, Tavistock.

Frank, J., 1949, *Law and the Modern Mind*, Stevens.

Freeman, 1985, 'Towards a Critical Theory of Family Law', *Current Legal Problems*, vol 38, p 153.

Galanter, M., 1992, 'Law Abounding: Legalisation Around the North Atlantic', *Modern Law Review*, vol 55, p 1.

Garfinkel, H., 1967, *Studies in Ethnomethodology*, Prentice Hall.

Geis, G., 1977, 'Rape in Marriage Reform', *Adelaide Law Review*, vol 6, p 284.

Ghandi, P.R. and MacNamee, E., 1991, 'The Family in UK Law and the International Covenant on Civil and Political Rights 1966', *International Journal of Law and the Family*, vol 5, p 104.

Ginzberg, N., *The Little Virtues*, Heinemann.

Gittins, D., 1985, *The Family in Question*, Macmillan.

Gilligan, C., 1982, *In a Different Voice*, Harvard University Press.

Glendon, M.A., 1977, *State, Law and Family*, North Holland Publishing Co.

Glendon, M.A., 1981, *The New Family and the New Property*, Butterworth.

Goffman, E., 1971, *The Presentation of Self in Everyday Life*, Penguin.

Golanty, E. and Harris, B., 1982, *Marriage and Family Life*, Houghton Mifflin.

Goodrich, P., 1990, *Languages of Law*, Weidenfeld and Nicholson.

Goodrich, P. and Hachamovitch, Y., 1991, 'Time Out of Mind: An Introduction to the Semiotics of Common Law', in P. Fitzpatrick (ed) *Dangerous Supplements*, Pluto Press.

Gordon, C., 1980, *Michel Foucault: Power/Knowledge*, Harvester Press.

Gould, T., 1983, *Inside Outsider, The Life and Times of Colin MacInnes*, Chatto and Windus.

Graycar, R., 1989, Equal Rights *Versus* Fathers' Rights, in C. Smart and S. Sevenhuijsen (eds) *Child Custody and the Politics of Gender,* Routledge.

Grbich, J., 1991, 'The Body in Legal Theory', in M.A. Fineman and N.S. Thomadsen (eds) *At The Boundaries of Law,* Routledge.

Griffiths, J., 1983, 'What Do Dutch Lawyers Actually Do in Divorce Cases?' *Law and Society Review,* vol 20, p 135.

Habermas, J., 1989, *The Structural Transformation of the Public Sphere,* MIT Press.

Hale, M., 1736, *Pleas of the Crown,* vol 1, Professional Books Reprint, 1971.

Hansard, HC, 1967–68, vol 758, col 830, HMSO.

Hansard, HL, 1968, vol 303, col 394, HMSO.

Hansard, HL, 1988, vol 502, col 490, HMSO.

Heidegger, M., 1977, *The Question Concerning Technology and Other Essays* (W. Lovitt, trans), Harper and Row.

Hekman, S.J., 1990, *Gender and Knowledge,* Polity Press.

Hobbes, T., 1966, *Leviathan,* in *The English Works of Thomas Hobbes,* Scientia Verlag Aalen.

Hoggett, B. and Pearl, D., 1987, *The Family, Law and Society,* 2nd ed, Butterworth.

Hume, 1797, *Criminal Law of Scotland,* Edinburgh.

Jones, D.P.H., 1987, 'The Evidence of a Three Year Old Child', *Criminal Law Review,* p 677.

Kennedy, D., 1982, 'Legal Education and the Reproduction of Hierarchy', *Journal of Legal Education,* vol 32, p 591.

King, M., 1991, Child Welfare Within Law: The Emergence of a Hybrid Discourse', *Journal of Law and Society,* vol 18, p 303.

King, M. and Piper, C., 1991, *How the Law Thinks about Children,* Gower.

Kymlicka, W., 1991, 'Rethinking the Family', *Philosophy and Public Affairs,* vol 20, p 77.

Landes, E. and Posner, R., 1978, 'The Economics of the Baby Shortage', *Journal of Legal Studies,* vol 7, p 323.

Lanham, D., 1983, 'Hale, Mysogyny and Rape' *Criminal Law Journal,* vol 7, p 148.

Lasch, C., 1977, *Haven in a Heartless World – The Family Under Siege,* Basic Books.

Law Commission, 1966, no 6, *The Field of Choice,* Cmnd 3123, HMSO.

Law Commission, 1970, no 33, *Nullity of Marriage,* HMSO.

Law Commission, 1985, no 146, *Polygamous Marriages,* Cmnd 9595, HMSO.

Law Commission, 1988, no 170, *Facing the Future, A Discussion Paper on the Ground for Divorce,* HMSO.

Law Commission, 1990, no 192, *The Ground for Divorce,* HMSO.

Law Commission, 1990, no 116, *Rape Within Marriage*, HMSO.

Law Comission, 1992, no 205, *Rape Within Marriage*, HMSO.

Lee, S., 1990, Changing the Province of Jurisprudence', in S. Lee and M. Fox (eds) *Learning Legal Skills*, Blackstone Press.

Locke, J., 1967, *Two Treatises of Government*, 2nd edn (ed P. Laslett) Cambridge University Press.

Luhmann, N., 1985, *A Sociological Theory of Law*, (trans E. King and M. Albrow) Routledge.

Luhmann, N., 1989, 'Law as Social System', *Northwestern University Law Review*, vol 83, p 136.

Lukes, S., 1991, *Moral Conflict and Politics*, Oxford University Press.

MacKinnon, C., 1987, *Feminism Unmodified*, Harvard University Press.

MacIntyre, A., 1981, *After Virtue – A Study in Moral Theory*, Duckworth.

Mallet, A. and Monier, J-C., 1992, 'Du droit des mineurs aux droits de l'enfant, *Esprit*, no 180, p 31.

Martin, J. and Roberts, C., 1984, *Women and Employment: A Lifetime Perspective*, HMSO.

Mauss, M., 1954, *The Gift* (trans I. Cunnison) Cohen and West.

Millham, S., Bullock, R., Hosie, K. and Little, M., 1989, *Access Disputes in Child-Care*, Gower.

Mitra, C.L., 1979, 'For She Has No Right or Power To Refuse Her Consent', *Criminal Law Review*, p 558.

Moran, L., 1990, 'A Study in the History of Male Sexuality in Law: Non-Consummation', *Law and Critique*, vol 1, p 155.

Morgan, D.H.J., 1977, *Introducing Sociology*, 2nd ed (ed P. Worsley).

Morgan, D.H.J., 1985, *The Family*, Routledge.

Mossman, M.J., 1986, 'Feminism and Legal Method: the Difference it Makes', *Australian Journal of Law and Society*, vol 3, p 30.

Mount, F., 1982, *The Subversive Family*, Jonathan Cape.

Naffine, N., 1990, *Law and the Sexes: Explorations in Feminist Jurisprudence*, Allen & Unwin.

Nielsen, L., 1990, 'Family Rights and the "Registered Partnership" in Denmark', *International Journal of Law and the Family*, vol 4, p 297.

Nozick, R., 1974, *Anarchy, State and Utopia*, Basic Books.

Oakley, A., 1974, *Housewife*, Penguin.

O'Donovan, K., 1979, 'The Male Appendage: Legal Definitions of Women', in S.B. Burman (ed) *Fitwork for Women*, Tavistock.

O'Donovan, K., 1985, *Sexual Division in Law*, Weidenfeld.

O'Donovan, K., 1986, 'Family Law and Legal Theory', in W.L. Twining (ed) *Legal Theory and Common Law*, Blackwell.

O'Donovan, K., 1989, 'Engendering Justice: Women's Perspectives and the Rule of Law', *University of Toronto Law Journal*, vol 39, p 127.

O'Donovan, K., 1991, 'Defences for Battered Wives Who Kill', *Journal of Law and Society*, vol 18, p 219.

Okin, S.M., 1989, *Justice, Gender and the Family*, Basic Books.

Okin, S.M., 1990, 'Feminism, the Individual and Contract Theory', *Ethics*, no 100, p 658.

Olsen, F., 1983, 'The Family and the Market', *Harvard Law Review*, vol 96, p 1497.

O'Neill, O., 1988, Children's Rights and Children's Lives', *Ethics*, no 98, p 445.

Pahl, J., 1989, *Money and Marriage*, Macmillan.

Pannick, D., 1987, *Judges*, Oxford University Press.

Parsons, T., 1949, *Essays in Sociological Theory*, Free Press.

Parsons, T., 1968, *American Sociology*, Basic Books.

Pateman, C., 1988a, *The Sexual Contract*, Polity Press.

Pateman, C., 1988b, 'The Fraternal Social Contract' in J. Keane (ed) *Civil Society and the State*, Verso.

Pearl, D., 1986, *Family Law and Immigrant Communities*, Jordan.

Phillips, A., 1991, 'Citizenship and Feminist Theory', in G. Andrews (ed) *Citizenship*, Lawrence and Wishart.

Pinchbeck, I., 1981, *Women Workers and the Industrial Revolution 1750–1850*, Virago.

Podmore, D. and Spencer, J., 1982, 'The Law as a Sex-Typed Profession', *Journal of Law and Society*, vol 9, p 21.

Polikoff, N., 1990, 'This Child Does Have Two Mothers: Redefining Parenthood to Meet the Needs of Children in Lesbian-Mother and Other Nontraditional Families', *Georgetown Law Journal*, vol 78, p 459.

Poulter, S., 1986, *English Law and Ethnic Minority Customs*, Butterworth.

Prichard, J.R.S., 1984, 'A Market for Babies?', *University of Toronto Law Journal*, vol 34, p 341.

Priest, J., 1984, 'Child of the Family', *Family Law*, vol 14, p 134.

Rawls, J., 1971, *A Theory of Justice*, Harvard University Press.

Reich, C., 1964, 'The New Property', *Yale Law Journal*, vol 73, p 733.

Report of the Home Office Advisory Group on Video Evidence, 1989, HMSO.

Report of the Inquiry into Child Abuse in Cleveland (Butler-Sloss), 1988, Cmnd 412, HMSO.

Richards, M., 1982, 'Post Divorce Arrangements for Children', *Journal of Social Welfare Law*, p 33.

Rights of Women, *Lesbian Mothers On Trial*, ROW, London.

Rorty, R., 1979, *Philosophy and the Mirror of Nature*, Princeton University Press.

Rose, N., 1987, 'Beyond the Public/Private Division: Law, Power and the Family', in P. Fitzpatrick and A. Hunt (eds) *Critical Legal Studies*, Blackwell.

Rousseau, J.J., 1986, *The Social Contract* (trans M. Cranston) Penguin Books.

Ryder, B., 1991, 'Straight Talk: Male Heterosexual Privilege', *Queen's Law Journal*, vol 16, p 287.

Sachs, A., and Wilson, J.H., 1978, *Sexism and the Law*, Martin Robertson.

Segal, L., 1990, *Slow Motion: Changing Masculinities, Changing Men*, Virago.

Seidler, V., 1988, 'Fathering, Authority and Masculinity' in R. Chapman and J. Rutherford (eds) 1988, *Male Order: Unwrapping Masculinity*, Lawrence and Wishart.

Seidler, V., 1989, *Rediscovering Masculinity*, Routledge.

Smart, C., 1984, *The Ties That Bind*, Routledge.

Smart, C., 1989a, *Feminism and the Power of Law*, Routledge.

Smart, C., 1989b, 'Power and the Politics of Child Custody' in C. Smart and S. Sevenhuijsen (eds) *Child Custody and the Politics of Gender*, Routledge.

Smart C., 1990, 'Law's Power, the Sexed Body and Feminist Discourse', *Journal of Law and Society*, vol 17, p 194.

Smith, J.C., 1984, comment on *R* v. *Caswell*, *Criminal Law Review*, 112.

Spencer, J. and Flin, R., 1990, *The Evidence of Children*, Blackstone.

Stanley, L., and Wise, S., 1983, *Breaking Out: Feminist Consciousness and Feminist Research*, Routledge.

Steel, M., 1990, *Lesbian Mothers, Custody Disputes and Court Welfare Reports*, University of East Anglia Social Work Reports.

Sugarman, D., 1986, 'Legal Theory, the Common LawMind and the Making of the Textbook Tradition', in W.L. Twining (ed) *Legal Theory and Common Law*, Blackwell.

Tasker, F. and Golombok, S., 1991, 'Children Raised by Lesbian Mothers – The Empirical Evidence', *Family Law*, vol 21, p 184.

Temkin, J., 1987, *Rape and the Legal Process*, Sweet and Maxwell.

Teubner, G., 1987a, 'Juridification – Concepts, Aspects, Limits, Solutions' in G. Teubner (ed) *Juridification of Social Spheres*, Walter de Gruyter.

Teubner, G., 1987b, *Autopoietic Law: A New Approach to Law and Society*, Walter de Gruyter.

Teubner, G., 1988, 'After Legal Instrumentalism' in G. Teubner (ed) *Dilemmas of Law in the Welfare State*, Walter de Gruyter.

Thèry, I., 1989, '"The Interest of the Child" and the Regulation of the Post-Divorce Family' in C. Smart and S. Sevenhuijsen (eds) *Child Custody and the Politics of Gender*, Routledge.

Thèry, I., 1992, 'Nouveaux droits de l'enfant, la potion magique', *Esprit*.

Thomas, P., 1991, 'Aids, Ideology and the Family', unpublished paper.

Thornton, M., 1986, 'Feminist Jurisprudence: Illusion or Reality?', *Australian Journal of Law and Society*, vol 3, p 5.

Thornton, M., 1989, 'Hegemonic Masculinity and the Academy', *International Journal of the Sociology of Law*, vol 17, p 115.

Wallerstein, J. and Kelly, J., 1980, *Surviving The Break-Up*, Bantam.

Wallerstein, J., and Blakeslee, S., 1986, *Second Chances – Men, Women and Children After a Decade of Divorce*, Bantam.

Weintraub, J., 1990, 'The Theory and Politics of the Public/Private Distinction', paper presented at the annual meeting of the American Political Science Association, San Francisco.

Weitzman, L., 1981, *The Marriage Contract*, Free Press.

Weitzman, L., 1985, *The Divorce Revolution*, Free Press.

West, R., 1988, 'Jurisprudence and Gender', *University of Chicago Law Review*, vol 55, p 1.

White, R., Carr, P. and Lowe, N., 1990, *A Guide to the Children Act 1989*, Butterworth.

Wilson, E., 1977, *Women and the Welfare State*, Tavistock.

Wilson, J.F., 1966, 'A Survey of Legal Education in the United Kingdom', *Journal of the Society of Public Teachers of Law*, vol ix, p 1.

Woolf, V., 1938, *Three Guineas*, Penguin.

Index